G

No Looking Back

GW00538347

David Thrower, 1927

No Looking Back

The story of a missionary to India

David Thrower

Grace Publications

GRACE PUBLICATIONS TRUST
139 Grosvenor Avenue,
London,
N5 2NH,
England.

© Grace Publications

First published 1986

ISBN 0 946462 09 7

Distributed by:
EVANGELICAL PRESS
16/18 High Street, Welwyn,
Hertfordshire, AL6 9EQ
England.

Typeset by Berea Press, Glasgow.
Printed in Great Britain by
        Cox & Wyman, Reading.

Contents

Preface

Using his memories and his diaries David Thrower wrote these reminiscences (his "story", as he called it) during the last few years of his life, at the suggestion of Chris Richards. He discussed what he had written with his grandson Paul Thrower, who proposed certain modifications, many of which were adopted. The material has been further reorganised for publication, but in such a way as to preserve almost all of what David wrote. The many short chapters have been combined to make fewer longer ones. Some material has been omitted where it was believed that it interrupted the flow of the narrative. Small changes in punctuation and in division of the text into paragraphs have also been made.

I wish to thank Paul Thrower, John Appleby and Wilfred Kuhrt who have each helped, in different ways, with the editorial work, and especially with the preparation of the introductions to each chapter, though the final responsibility remains my own.

Paul Helm.
Formby.
June 1986.

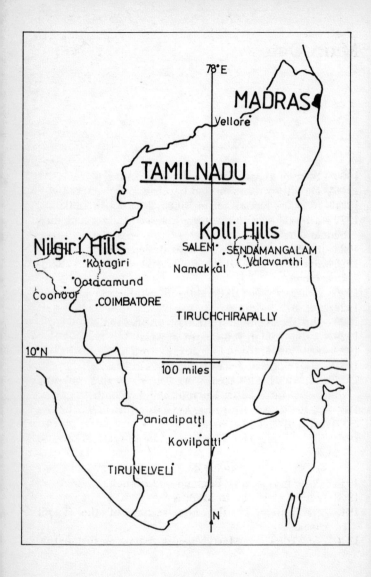

Main Dates

1900 – birth of David Thrower on 9th January
1916 – David's conversion and baptism
1921 – he offers himself for missionary service in India
1922 – arrival in India, settling first in Madras and then Sendamangalam
1923 – he begins work on a Tamil Bible concordance
1925 – marriage to Martena (Marty) Watts on 22nd December
1926 – death of their first child, Olive in December
1927 – return to Madras
1929 – the Throwers' first furlough to England
1929 – a son, Vivian John, born in April
1929 – return to India in October, to work in the Kolli Hills
1931 – a second son, Irwin Jesse, born in March
1932 – Marty's health breaks. An extended vacation in the summer is followed by her return to England
1933 – David returns to India. Marty's return is delayed by ill-health until mid-1934
1935 – in February the Throwers move from Namakkal to Madras
    – birth of a daughter, Olive
1939 – March, return to England on furlough
1940 – return to India, to Madras
1943 – publication of the first section of the Tamil concordance
1946 – breakdown of Marty's health. Home on furlough

1947 – David returns alone to India, to the Salem area

1947 – Indian Home Rule established, in August

1948 – Death of Gandhi in January. David returns to Madras

1950 – the Republic of India is established, 26th January

1950 – publication of the second section of the Tamil concordance

1952 – following another break-down in David's health, furlough in England

1953 – David returns to India

1956 – Marty returns to England

1958 – David returns to England

1959 – the Throwers resume work in India

1960 – visit of E F Kevan
     – publication of the first complete edition of the Tamil concordance

1964 – furlough in England

1965 – return to India. In June David indicates his desire to retire

1968 – David begins to help Tamil-speakers of Malaysia

1968 – visit to Malaya, September-December
     – David retires from full-time missionary service

1970 – furlough in England

1970-1 – a second visit to Malaya

1980 – death of Marty Thrower, in November

1982 – David's last visit to England

1985 – death of David Thrower.

Introduction

First appearances sometimes deceive us. The following pages contain the story of a remarkable man, a fine Christian missionary. But the story is not what you might expect. There is no account here of great preaching, of the opening up of new fields for the gospel, of doctrinal controversy or of vigorous church growth. There is no dramatic pioneering, no great acts of missionary statesmanship. During David Thrower's life there was some of all these things in India. But it is not recorded here. And yet this is the record of a first-rate missionary. How can this be?

To begin with, while this is the story of David Thrower, it is David Thrower's own story; a few fragments from a long life of over sixty years – sixty years – of missionary service in India. David was extremely self-effacing. He was unassuming and undemonstrative. He took each day as it came. As a consequence he tended to play down important events and to play up small ones. A snake crawling along the roof during a service is recorded as if it were as important as the preaching itself or as the devastating floods in Madras. David was not given to being dramatic, or to exaggerating for effect. His God was the God of truth who has all events under his control. So in what follows there is no emphasis upon the first person singular. It is necessary to read between the lines to appreciate the personal cost and commitment in David's life.

But then why publish his story? If there is no soul-stirring stuff about the advance of the kingdom, no mass conversions, no record of theological conquest or savagery subdued by grace, what is there in it for us? What is remarkable about David's story – worth recording and worth knowing about – is what it reveals about Christian virtue and character. In particular, it is worth looking out for the following themes.

The general attitude of Christian missionaries in India during this period was *paternalistic*. Indian Christians were not treated by the missionaries as believers of equal standing, whatever may have been believed in theory about the equality of all Christians before God. Almost unconsciously missionary work in India came to be regarded as part of the British Raj. As a result Indian Christians were allowed to take little or no responsibility for themselves. They did not mature, but expected all important decisions to be taken by the Europeans. And the Europeans obliged. David and his wife Marty were among the relatively few who, from the start of their work, came to see things differently.

They treated the Indians as equals. They were patient and offered help without condescension. The help they gave was always with the aim of getting the Indian Christians to help themselves, to develop skills, to gain in confidence, to become self-reliant and ulimately to form and govern churches for themselves. This help was given in ways which may seem small and commonplace to us. For example, David taught several men to type and to drive in order that they could get work and support their families. Marty taught sewing skills, cookery, hygiene and animal husbandry.

It is tempting to dismiss this as 'social work' and to ask 'Where's the gospel?' But in an environment hostile to the Christian faith it was necessary to develop a Christian

culture which is at one and the same time in harmony with
India and yet distinctively Christian. The only way to
achieve this was to get Indians to think for themselves.
Preaching the gospel is not a separate, isolated activity in
India any more than it was for Christ, who went about
doing good, or for the Apostles. Yet such practical work did
not take the place of the declaring of the word of life. Quite
apart from the value of such help in itself the aim was to
provide a setting for the gospel – 'pre-evangelism' at a time
before that ugly word was invented.

Look out as well for the way in which David attempted to
use the novel situations into which they came in new and
creative ways to benefit their Christian work. The Pauline
'all things to all men' has come to suggest weakness and
lack of principle. But for Paul this was his way of making an
initiative for the gospel, bending and adapting those
matters which are secondary and non-essential to gain a
hearing for the essential gospel. David Thrower had the
spiritual alertness to be adaptable in a situation in which a
refusal to change could result in grinding disappointment
and disillusionment. David did not inherit this attitude
from the churches from which he came, nor from his
missionary forerunners, highly as he regarded both. He
thought things out for himself from scratch.

David kept to his course for over sixty years. It seems to
have been impossible to discourage him (though there
surely must have been times when he was discouraged). He
was tenacious, with both feet on the ground. It was not that
he was unaware of the difficulties, living in an ivory tower.
Rather his tenacity showed itself in the practical details over
which he took great pains. A vivid but typical example of
this is the way in which he could not rest content with a
working knowledge of Tamil. He was never without his
notebook, recording unusual phrases or ways of speaking.
He set himself high, exacting standards. Though out of the

limelight he lived in the gaze of his Master to whom he
knew he was unanswerable.

At present Christians seem to get discouraged easily. It is
common to hear talk of 'vision' but much less common to
find those who stick to a task. No doubt there are many
reasons for this present failure. But no one who reads David
Thrower's reminiscences and reflects on his long life of
service can doubt that it is possible, with God's help, to live
in a way that is utterly dependable through thick and thin.
The details of David's life, and the particular features of his
personality, are not to be copied. But his determination, his
willingness to endure hardness, should be an inspiration to
all who care for God's glory.

Perhaps one secret of this determination is that God gave
to David an orderly, methodical frame of mind. Like Paul,
he did not shadow-box. He was disciplined, in the use of his
time and money, in keeping his diary, in answering letters
in keeping to time. So there was no magic formula, but a
sturdy Calvinistic piety governed by a sense of joyful,
thankful obligation to Christ who had loved him and given
himself for him.

In all this David may seem an old-fashioned figure, so
used have we become to a permissive and casual attitude to
affairs in the Christian church, and so used to physical
comfort. But the maintenance of the gospel, at any time and
place, and its success, depend, under God, on the
willingness of Christians to keep at their posts of duty in all
weathers, when no one else notices, aware that the eye of
God is on us and that we have a great work to do. David
Thrower was never, as far as one can tell, in the headlines.
He was not a Whitefield or a Spurgeon. This did not matter
to him. He had no illusions. But he kept to his God-
appointed calling with cheerful and methodical devotion,
through family upheavals, sickness and great changes in the
Mission and in the life of India. He endured to the very end.

David was not a great theological thinker. There is no evidence that he revelled in Augustine or Calvin or Jonathan Edwards. His writings, apart from the monumental achievement of the Tamil concordance, were on the practical and devotional side. Some may be prepared to criticise him for this. What India needed – and needs – they may say, is doctrine, clear Christian truth clearly presented.

Perhaps so; David Thrower, in all likelihood, would not have dissented from this. But he also recognised his own limitations. He was not trained or equipped for the work of a theological thinker, and he knew it. He clearly made a careful assessment of his own abilities and gifts and lived and worked accordingly.

Yet though he was not a creative theological thinker, he was a doer. Though he could not lecture long and learnedly on the decrees of God or the inspiration of Scripture or the nature of saving faith, by God's help he could and did take God at his word, and trust him implicitly. Not only when affairs were going well, but when the going was tough; when there was personal bereavement, crippling ill-health, faithlessness in others, a flood, a beating-up. All such events, as though by a mysterious chemical process, became opportunities for David and Marty to exercise and re-exercise trust in God, to renew his commitment to what he was convinced was God's life-long call.

It is easy to be captivated by a romantic picture of the missionary which bears little or no relation to the facts. And equally easy to react in the opposite direction and to think that the missionary is a super saleman – the missionary according to Hollywood or the management consultant. But missionary work, as all Christian work, is hard grind. The life of David Thrower – and these remarkable self-effacing reminiscences of the octogenarian David which now follow – are a sharp and yet welcome reminder of the continuing needs of missionary work, and of the fact that the Lord is still able to grant gifts of kindly wisdom and gritty determination to men and women to enable the work of the kingdom to go forward.

Paul Helm

There was no particular reason to think that David was marked out for missionary work. He was an ordinary lad, from an ordinary church background. He had no voices or visions. But as a young Christian, converted when he was 16, he made the most of his opportunities. He developed skills in shorthand, and learned to take responsibility. God's providence is visible to us in all this, in his godly background, in the acquiring of abilities which would later be of use in translation and other literary work. And the leading of God's providence soon became apparent to David through his firm conviction that he ought to be a missionary to India.

That conviction was to be tested. Out of duty and love to Christ he offered himself to the Mission. He was young, and with no formal theological education. He was turned down. Though staggered by this, his resolve to go to India intensified. "I told them that by this time the conviction had deepened to such an extent that I intended to go and should go to India, because the Lord had need of me there. In due time I was accepted for service". He went with the support of the people of God and especially that of his own church, Courland Grove Clapham. "I have pleaded for the prayers of friends, for without them I cannot get along with any degree of joy in service; and I should like to say how much I appreciate the kindness of many friends who have written assuring me of their prayers".

After a few months of hurried preparation, David sailed for India in 1922, aged 22. Tamil India was to be the scene of his life's work.

1.
Setting course

My paternal forefathers of at least the last four generations left me with a godly heritage for which I am profoundly thankful. Some were associated with their parish churches, while others were members of the Baptist church founded in the village of Horham in Mid-Suffolk in 1799. I remember visiting my great-grandfather David Thrower and his wife with Dad one summer when I was very young. He died when I was seven years old but great-grandma survived him for a few years during which I visited her. The eldest of David's children was my grandfather William who spent nearly all his life in Horham.

Originally a "thrower" was a person engaged in converting raw silk into silk threads; a silk thrower. I do not know whether any of my ancestors were silk-throwers but by grandfather William's time at any rate they were farm labourers. However, grandfather had an edge over some of his fellows in that he was horseman for a farmer. He had the care of his master's horses and thus was responsible for the supply of energy for traction on the farm. He never earned more than about twelve shillings a week, and I think his family could not indulge in tea. They are said to have toasted bread until it was black and crumbled it into hot water as a substitute.

By that time the drift of the labour force from rural to urban areas had set in. Therefore, hoping his eldest son Arthur William might enjoy an easier life than he himself had experienced, grandfather sent him, a lad of fifteen, to London. Arthur then started work as assistant to a relative who was coachman to a doctor in Clapham. In 1895 he secured a post at one of London's largest bakeries located in Battersea; a post that he held for forty-five years. The same year he married Mary Ann Fincham and on 9th January 1900 she presented him with a son whom they called David Arthur.

Dad not only earned his living at the bakery but also served another Master as a keen worker at a Baptist chruch in Clapham. He was also on a number of committees, including the Strict Baptist Mission Council. In the course of time he was appointed an elder of his church and superintendent of the Sunday School. At Sunday worship he led the "service of praise", announcing the hymns and, for many years while the church had no organ, sounded the opening note on a "pitch-pipe".

We lived in Clapham not far from where Clapham North Underground station now stands. On reaching the school-going age of five I crossed an elevated railway near our house by a footbridge to attend school. During the summer holidays Dad took me to one of our relatives' homes in Suffolk while Mother, who suffered from a heart complaint and could not travel, stayed in London. I remember Mother as kind and gentle, although rather frail. One day she helped me to cut out cardboard figures of a camel and other animals depicted on our tea-caddy.

Owing to Mother's failing health, Dad placed me with a maiden aunt, in the hamlet of Wilby, Suffolk, where I attended the village school. A son of the village blacksmith was my special pal; we usually spent the long holidays harvesting the grass on a plot behind the forge. Mother left us for the Better Land before the end of the year.

On Sundays Aunt and I walked to Horham Baptist Chapel two miles away to attend the morning and afternoon services. On one occasion I spoke to the minister about something in his ministry that was a blessing to me. Although only about eight years old I evidently had begun awakening to my need of the salvation that he preached.

Aunt Emma was postwoman for the parish and I accompanied her on her delivery round every morning before school. During the latter part of my time there I was permitted to assist in delivering the mail. But when Dad joined us for his summer holiday in 1910 a new crisis hit us; Aunt informed Dad that her health was failing and she could not keep me any longer. Dad had no alternative; he had to take me back to Battersea, thus terminating the happiest period of my childhood.

How different life was in London from what I had known in Wilby and how much the great city had changed since I left it four years earlier! Here in town we had gas for light and cooking; there it was oil for light and coal for cooking. Incidentally, our gas was from plain gas jets with no incandescent mantles. In Wilby there was no public transport; but here electric tramways were coming into existence and cabs were beginning to dispense with horses and go over to petrol. Electricity had not yet been brought into homes but was replacing other types of lighting in the streets. Where gas was still used for street lighting the lamp-lighter was needed to light and extinguish the lamps.

As my fourteenth birthday approached Dad informed me that he, a poor working man, could not afford to give me any further education; I must leave school and seek employment. However, in the event I continued at school for a couple of months longer, while Dad made enquiries among his workmates at the bakery regarding a possible job for me. A couple of months after I reached school-leaving-age (fourteen years) Dad heard of an office-boy's job in the chambers of three elderly barristers just off Fleet Street in the City. I applied to the gentlemen and was informed that

I could have the post, the pay being eight shillings a week (40p). I was further told that I would be the first lad to receive so much, that the duties would be very light and leave me much spare time which I must use profitably. I undertook to teach myself Pitman's shorthand in my spare time in the office, which I did and then translated column after column from the newspaper for practice of my new skill. My only companion in the office was a middle-aged clerk who had to write all legal documents by hand as the office had no typewriter; in fact there weren't many of those about at that time. I frequently had to attend the Law Courts nearby with an armful of tomes for one of my employers; sometimes those visits were intensely interesting. For instance, one of our clients was the defendant in a case brought by the mighty London County Council. The Council wished to widen the Strand and put down tracks for electric trams, but our client owned a hotel in the Strand and was not willing to sell the property to the LCC. Hence the case was taken to the High Court to compel the Hotelier to co-operate with the Council's scheme. 'We' won the case for the defendant; trams never ran along the Strand.

Apart from learning shorthand there was no way for me to improve my position at that office. If only the place had a typewriter! So before the year was out I began to look for a more suitable post, and early in 1915 got into an insurance broker's office in the Haymarket. There I became acquainted with various types of office routine and soon obtained permission to practise on the typewriter when it was not in use. Thus it wasn't long before I filled the typist's place when he took time off. Before I had been in the Haymarket twelve months I began looking at the "Wanted" column of the newspaper once more; this time I sought a shorthand-typist's post. My first application was a failure, but the second succeeded; in June 1916 I joined the office of the North Metropolitan Power Company in their power station at Harlesden, North West London. There I worked as shorthand-typist and general clerk.

I cannot pinpoint the date of my conversion; but it appears that God worked in my heart from the time that I spoke to the pastor of the Horham Baptist church about something in one of his sermons when I was a boy. Nothing else of significance happened until I was sixteen; but I regularly attended Sunday services with Dad after returning from Wilby. However, in June 1916 I began to feel it was time I made a public stand for the Lord. I therefore decided to apply to the Baptist church for believer's baptism and church membership. As Dad was a deacon of the church I mentioned the matter to him while we were walking home after service one Sunday. When I asked him whether I could be baptised he promptly replied in the words of Philip the evangelist in response to a similar enquiry: "If thou believest with all thine heart thou mayest"

I sent a formal application to the Church Secretary, after which I was interviewed by the deacons, then I was asked to give my testimony at a gathering of the members of the church. They accepted my brief work of witness to the saving goodness of God, and my baptism by immersion took place on Sunday 23 July 1916. Martena Watts, who later became my wife, was baptised and joined the same church the previous year. We worked together in the Sunday School and held hands under the table during the weekly lesson preparation class. Not long after Marty and I became boy/girl friends we started a practice that was to prove one of the most blessed things we did in our lifetime together. We read an American tract on the subject of proportionate giving with the result that we decided to pay God's tithes and give our offerings. We also opened an account in which we kept a record of our giving, calling it The Lord's Fund. This account we maintained throughout our married life. In fact I still keep it. In our experience the Lord has graciously fulfilled His promises recorded in Proverbs 3:10: "Honour the Lord with your wealth, with the firstfruits of all your crops; then your barns will be filled to overflowing, and your vats will brim over with new wine." And Malachi 3:10: "Bring the whole tithe into the storehouse, that there may be food in my house. Test me in this, says the Lord Almighty, and see if I will not throw open the floodgates of heaven and pour out so much blessing that you will not have room enough for it."

The blessing that has flowed from this act of obedience on our part has been incalculable; for this I thank Him with all my heart. In addition, at that period I was often conscious of God's leading and help in my everyday life.

In January 1918, at eighteen years of age, I became subject to compulsory service in either the army or navy. A deacon of our church was a retired naval man and he urged me to join the Royal Navy. I applied for service with the Navy at Chatham and my application was accepted. Then I returned to the Power Station and reported my action to the manager; I told him the date that I had been told to join up and start my naval training. The manager wrote to the relevant officer at Chatham and explained that he could not release me from the office until he secured a suitable replacement, the power station being an essential wartime plant producing power for a number of ordnance factories. The officer readily permitted the company to retain my services for two months during which time a Jewish lad was appointed in my place; I then left Harlesden and reported to Chatham barracks.

I became one of fifty-two lads living in a wooden hut and undergoing training as Ordinary Seaman under the supervision of a Petty Officer who occupied a room at one end of the hut. We wore the cap band of HMS Pembroke. In addition to the instruction given in the barracks we were taken to warships in the dockyard for lessons in gunnery.

On Sunday mornings those of us who wished to attend a place of worship were marched into the town; there we dispersed to Anglican, Methodist, Baptist, and other churches. The folk at the Baptist chapel that I attended gave me a warm welcome and one family in particular opened their home to me on my evenings off.

After a few months training we were liable to be drafted to a ship bound for any part of the world. Of the fifty-two men in my hut I was probably the only one who was not assigned to a vessel, and that was undoubtedly due to God's hand on my life. Had I gone on draft I would almost certainly not have started my Indian career when I did. One of my hut-mates was put into the Barracks Office but the work was not to his liking; he longed to be sent to a ship. Learning of this I offered to take his place; the exchange was approved and I joined the office staff while the other chap went to sea.

In the autumn the German defence began to crack and the Kaiser capitulated early in November. The Armistice took effect at the eleventh hour on the eleventh day of the eleventh month and demobilisation began almost immediately. I was one of the most highly favoured, for I went home in January 1919 with a huge bag containing my kit on my shoulder.

Back in my post at the Power Station I soon found suitable digs not far from my work and saved much time and expense in travel. Then I began to attend evening classes at a branch of Pitman's Commercial College in Kilburn. There I practised high speed shorthand, eventually reaching one hundred and seventy words a minute; I also studied accountancy and French. Towards the close of that year one of the shorthand tutors resigned; I applied for his post and got it. My duties comprised teaching five days a week and three evenings from 6.30 to

9.00 pm. Unfortunately my work necessitated giving up shorthand speed practice for I was very keen to secure the much-coveted Pitman's silver medal for writing accurately at two hundred words a minute.

Shortly afterwards, the authorities at the headquarters of Pitman's in Southampton Row offered me a six-months correspondence course of tuition to prepare me for their Shorthand Teacher's Diploma examination. I did the course and took the examination early in 1920. The latter was by no means a walkover but comprised six difficult tests one of which was to give a lesson with blackboard illustrations to the examiners. However, by God's help I secured the Diploma at the first attempt, something that almost half the examinees usually failed to do. Thus I became the only qualified shorthand tutor on the staff of the Kilburn branch. I became a member of the National Union of Teachers.

I usually cycled from Battersea to Kilburn, having left my lodgings in Willesden. Being a forgetful young fellow I once paid dearly for the weakness. During an evening session the headmaster came to my classroom to ask me to fasten the windows throughout the three-storey building at closing time as he would be leaving early. Alas, I forgot this chore until I had reached home six miles away and finished my supper. In my distress of mind I consulted Dad who was on night duty at the bakery; I then decided that there was nothing for it but to return to Kilburn, enter College by one of the ground-floor windows, then close and bolt the windows of all the rooms. My bike was out of order, so I had to go by bus, reaching Kilburn a little before midnight. I took the precaution of finding a policeman on street patrol and told him. I didn't want to be arrested for the break-in I was about to commit! Then I carried out my plan and secured all the windows but one in the college. My punishment ended when I arrived home at 2.30 am after walking home the six miles, all public transport having disappeared.

In March 1920 I noticed in the Strict Baptist Mission Herald an appeal for a young man to serve as assistant to Mr E A Booth in Madras who was in Britain on sick leave. The doctor was only ready to approve of his returning to the tropics if he was given an assistant, and desire to serve in this way began to work powerfully within me. Meanwhile my fiancee, Marty, was sure that she had been called to serve overseas, but had not told me lest I might be "called" by her instead of by the Lord. She hoped and prayed that I would read that appeal in the Herald and be led to respond to it. A few weeks later I attended a missionary rally at which Mr Booth made a stirring appeal for an assistant. That led to my making application for service in India with the Mission. Another young man also responded to the appeal and the Mission Council interviewed both of us the same evening during the summer of that year, but for different reasons both of us failed to convince the members of the Council that we had received a divine call to the work.

However, I intended to apply again later, but in the meantime, wished to learn from this set-back. I began to read every book I could lay hands on dealing with foreign missionary service. As I had no preaching experience I sought opportunities for this type of ministry, and Marty's brother, Newman Watts, was a great help to me in this connection. He was an itinerant preacher with more engagements than he felt he could properly fulfil; so he kindly arranged for me to take over a few of them in churches in the Home Counties. These were all Sunday services which I was able to conduct without interfering with my work at Pitman's. One church that I visited in this way was in the village of Potten End, Berkhamsted, Herts. I became friendly with several folk there, friendships which have lasted throughout my career. One such friend who still lives in the village remembers me as "the little boy preacher", for those days I looked more like a lad of sixteen than a man of twenty. The trepidation with which I began this work was at times agonising. For instance, I "preached" at a church in Kings Langley, Herts., on the last Sunday in 1920, unhappy memories of which effort have haunted me ever since!

About the end of 1920 I submitted my second application to the SBM and, when interviewed, told Council that I was called to serve the Lord in India; to India I should go, whether with the SBM or not. This time Council agreed to accept me providing the doctor considered me fit for work in the tropics. Just before Easter 1921 I resigned from my work at College and spent the following six weeks in such pursuits as Bible study and the reading of missionary biographies.

As I did not look very healthy the medical examination was considered particularly important in my case. It was, therefore, decided that the Mission President should accompany me when I went to the doctor; his consulting rooms were in Harley Street, London. After giving me a thorough overhaul the physician announced the verdict: "Mr Thrower will probably do better health-wise in the tropics than in Britain but his throat is in a bad state. I therefore, recommend that you take him to an old friend of mine across the road who is an Ears, Nose and Throat specialist."

In due course the Secretary of Council went with me to see the specialist; he confirmed that my tonsils needed to be removed and offered to perform the operation himself. Shortly afterwards he relieved me of both tonsils and adenoids.

That day I had waited for so long finally dawned; it was 6th May 1921, the date of the monthly SBM Council

meeting. On that day, Dad, who was a member, took me
with him and parked me in an ante-room. During the
meeting he was asked to call me in. The President informed
me that I had been unanimously accepted as a worker of the
Mission, gave me the customary hand-shake of welcome
and said, "You have just started on a very long furrow and,
you know, he that puts his hand to the plough and turns
back is not fit for the work."

By that time it was almost the middle of the year; Mr and
Mrs Booth were due to leave for India in December; it was,
therefore, not possible for me to take a full course of
training. However, I went to Livingstone Medical College
at Whipps Cross, Leytonstone for the remainder of the
current course and a couple of months of the next one, after
the summer recess. For me that was an instructive and
interesting time, with lectures interspersed with practical
work at two London hospitals. Dr Tom Jays, a former
missionary in Dar-es-Salaam, East Africa, made an ideal
Principal; he gave his students as good a general medical
training as possible, including adequate advice regarding
their own health in the tropics. The course enabled
missionaries to render simple medical aid to folk in rural
areas of many countries. I was at Livingstone until the
beginning of December; then spent a hectic week
purchasing tropical kit and packing my bags.

Several folk still thought, however, even at this stage,
that I was unsuited to the work ahead of me, and I recall
one asserting most strongly, "David is running before he
has been sent; he will be back within three years, finished
with India."

That friend lived to a great age and, when we met many
years later, laughingly admitted his error of judgement in
1921. However, our farewell was held in London early in
December, during which Mr Booth made a rousing appeal
for more missionaries to serve in Tamilnadu. On 9th

December we boarded the P & O mail steamer "Malwa" at Tilbury. I was, of course, full of excitement. In the immediate future lay an ocean voyage that was certain to be packed with interest. Beyond that was my life-work in a new country, a strange language and culture.

While the New Year mail was being unloaded in Bombay we had a drive around part of the great city in a horse-drawn four-wheeler. The ship was bound for the Far East and we were booked to Colombo; so we returned to the "Malwa" and left Bombay that evening. The vessel proceeded South to Cape Comorin and there turned eastward, entering Colombo harbour the morning of 3rd January 1922.

We had been aboard three and a half weeks; a wonderful time for me, looking for flying fish, dolphins, porpoises, a spouting whale or even a shark following the ship. But it was not all fun; Mr Booth was my first Tamil pundit, who taught me the whole of the script of the language during the voyage. I learned the 246 characters with their pronunciation, which include 18 consonants and 216 consonant-vowel combinations.

Before leaving the docks we three bound for India contacted Thomas Cook's representative and asked him to make rail bookings with sleeping accommodation for us on the night train to Talaimannar in the north of the Island. He did the business for us by telephone from the wharf. We spent most of the day seeing a few places of interest in the beautiful city of Colombo. We had lunch at an English hotel and I was introduced to the tropical fruit pappaya or paw-paw which I found pleasant and refreshing, in the heat of Ceylon. In the evening the three of us went to the railway station in good time and enquired for our berths on the train. Then I struck the snag of the day. A coupé had been reserved for Mr and Mrs Booth, but a berth had not been booked for D A Thrower; furthermore there wasn't one available for him! I did not relish the prospect of sitting up all night. However, the relevant railway official tried to be helpful; he informed us that, although a man named Daghoomer had booked the only other sleeping berth on the train, there was the possibility that he would not travel that day; in the event I could have his berth. The incident ended happily when this occurred and we realised that the name Daghoomer was a garbled version of D A Thrower resulting from our order being telephoned from the noisy quay at the docks. Many years after a lady missionary at Ootacamund suffered a still more embarrassing situation of this kind. A Miss Tencate went to "Ooty" Station on the Nilgiri Hills and made a booking for travel from the main rail terminus on the plains. When she later reached the main line station and looked for her berth "it was not". Then she learned that the reservations clerk was at a loss to know what to do about the telegram he had received; it read: "Please reserve for ten cats"!!

Early the next morning the train ran on to the jetty at Talaimannar and we boarded the ferry steamer bound for the Indian mainland. After a two-and-a-half hours crossing we pulled alongside the pier at Dhanushkodi the southern terminal of the Madras railway line. After immigration and customs formalities had been attended to we found our respective compartments on the Madras train standing a few yards away. There was no hitch this time. The last four hundred of our seven thousand mile journey took about twenty hours; we arrived in Madras early on 5th January 1922 and were met by Miss Ruth Appleby and Lincoln Watts. The last stage of my long trip from Battersea to Kilpauk, Madras, was made in a horse-drawn carriage; as we turned into a certain street Mr Booth announced: "We are now in Kilpauk".

At the Mission House Lincoln's wife, Ethel, introduced me to my room at the rear of the building. One of its windows revealed a striking Indian rural scene that included a huge mass of ten feet high prickly pear cactus and the mud and thatch huts of an outcast village. My first day was mainly spent unpacking my gear and settling in. In the evening, however, I cycled with Lincoln to a prayer meeting at the Ayanapuram village a mile or so away. Although I did not understand the proceedings it was a joy to meet a group of Tamil Baptist friends the day I arrived in Madras. The high and rapidly rising temperature was one of my early impressions of Madras. I was also amazed at the very large rooms and high roofs of European bungalows and the number of servants employed by Westerners.

The first Protestant missionaries to India, German Lutherans, arrived in 1706, working at the Danish settlement in Tranquebar. They aimed to translate the Word of God into Tamil, to preach for conversions to Christ and to encourage the formation of self-governing churches. The New Testament was translated in 1714. About eighty years later William Carey arrived in Bengal, sent by English Particular Baptists. He came from humble beginnings but had the same exalted aims as the Lutherans. His pioneering work caught the imagination of the English-speaking Christian world.

David Thrower was in this tradition of mission. He described his first efforts at learning Tamil as "beginning to roll the great stone uphill". But he did not remain content with an elementary grasp of the language. He took a number of examinations, some of them on his own initiative, passing with distinction. He asked Tamils to note his mistakes when preaching so that he could gain a complete mastery. He became fluent in the language and in increasing demand as a speaker.

Although not theologically gifted David was convinced of the doctrines of grace and God developed in him a quiet, calm and persistent Christian commitment to the Tamils. "The midnight darkness can only be dispelled by the light of the gospel of Jesus Christ," he wrote. He was convinced of the need of Christian literature in Tamil and set to work on the mammouth task of preparing a topical Bible concordance in Tamil. But the Mission was not enthusiastic. As a consequence David had to pay for secretarial help out of his own pocket. But David kept at it . . .

David was married to Marty Watts in December, 1925. Her brother Lincoln was already a missionary colleague. The tragedy of the loss of their first child, Olive, followed. But such setbacks seem to have strengthened the Throwers' already steely resolve. Their loss enabled them to comfort others similarly placed. Their reaction to this providence had a steadying influence upon their fellow-missionaries.

2.
Uphill

Now I had to become acquainted with the Tamil people and learn their language. The Tamils are short of stature and very dark-skinned; in fact some are almost black. Their dress is quite different from that of Westerners. The men, particularly in rural areas, wear as their main garment a length of cloth tied round their waist and reaching to the ankles; this is called a "dhoti". In the 1920's many of the village men wore no upper garment but, if they could afford it, had a short length of cloth which they folded and hung over their left shoulder; a multi-purpose scarf-cum-handkerchief. Men in urban areas usually wear a shirt, the tail of which hangs outside the dhoti. Tamil women wear the sari as their chief garment. This is a length of cloth six or eight yards long in a seemingly endless variety of colours and designs. It is tied round the waist and reaches almost to the ground, covering the feet. The women also usually wear a skirt under their sari. One end of the sari is kept loose and hung over the left shoulder. All women except those who are extremely poor also wear a tightly fitting blouse, often called a jacket. The food of the Tamils consists mainly of rice which, being a starchy cereal, leaves much to be desired as the staple article of diet. Many varieties of curry are eaten by those who can afford such luxuries; the food is invariably highly spiced and salted. By temperament these people are docile, patient and friendly. Generally speaking they are very religious Hindus but also remarkably tolerant towards those of other faiths.

The day after my arrival, Lincoln and I cycled to the National Bank of India, where I opened a personal account that I still operate. We also called on Mr Venkatachariar, a well-known Tamil pundit, who agreed to start giving me lessons immediately. Thus I commenced one of the toughest mental disciplines to be found anywhere; I was attempting to gain a working knowledge of the world's second most difficult language. My pundit was so popular that he could only give his students a one-hour lesson daily. He was kept busy in this way from soon after daybreak until the evening. My fellow students included anglican, congregational, lutheran and methodist missionaries. Our tutor was an outstanding Tamil grammarian who had for many years studied the needs of foreign students of the language and developed a highly efficient teaching technique. Although good Tamil grammars were in general use this pundit dispensed with all such aids and taught his own system. He provided copious blackboard material for us to copy and later study at home. In this way he gave us in one hour enough to keep us busy for five or six hours of homework. His method was to teach the elements of Tamil grammar to a beginner during the first six weeks. Then he would start work on the books set for tranlation in the syllabus for the first annual examination.

In March, Lincoln and Ethel Watts left Madras for furlough and I remember that the day they left for Bombay the thermometer reached ninety seven degrees fahrenheit in the shade. As it was only the beginning of the hot season I wondered how much higher the mercury would rise during the coming months.

By August I began to feel my Tamil study was too difficult for me and suffered much depression on that account. However, by God's help, I slowly got a grip on my subject and duly sat for the first examination in November. An attack of fever nearly prevented my doing so; I also had the handicap of having spent only ten and a half months studying the full year's course. But by the goodness of the Lord I succeeded in securing a pass in all sections of both written and oral divisions. This first hurdle surmounted, I prepared to give my first public address in Tamil at the Watchnight Service at our Vepery church on New Years Eve. In the event I took the chair and also spoke for fifteen minutes. As the building was filled to capacity my debut was somewhat of an ordeal.

The SBM gave new missionaries the whole of their first year for language study, but during their second year expected them to engage in such work as would help them to acquire practical knowledge of the vernacular. Priority would still have to be given to preparation for the Second Tamil Examination.

From the beginning of 1923 I occasionally conducted a service at one of the churches and I recollect my consternation when Miss Ruth Appleby (a missionary colleague) walked into the chapel as I was about to commence my first ever Sunday service in Tamil. During that year I also conducted weekly prayer meetings at three other meeting places in the area.

A Tamil congregation comprises the men sitting on one side of the building and women on the other with an aisle between the two groups. The pastor and guest speaker, if any, sit on chairs or a bench at the front, often but not always on a raised platform. The congregation is seated on grass mats on the floor. A crowd of children sit in front of the adults, but on the bare mud or concrete floor. A bench is usually provided on either side of the front door for the use of any distinguished visitors present. In very large towns and cities the grass mats are replaced by wooden benches. Where floor mats are used the worshippers remain seated during the singing of the hymns. Just before the offering a common sight is that of a youngster scuttling across the church, sent by mum to get a coin from dad for her to put in the collecting bag.

Those who attended these gatherings were, on the whole, very patient with the budding preacher, but it was evident that at least some of them found my effusions boring!

Our summer vacation away from the heat of the plains was usually spent on the Nilgiri Hills three hundred and sixty miles south west of Madras. That year, however, I took my holiday on the Kolli Hills in Salem District, where Lincoln and Ethel were stationed. Their headquarters was situated at an altitude of three thousand seven hundred feet; the climate was, therefore, comparatively cool. While I was with them, Lincoln and Ethel took me to several of the meeting places on the Kollis. On one of these occasions we made a tour of two widely separated villages, staying in the Mission school buildings in each place. This provided excellent opportunities for unhurried conversation as we walked over the hills. On one of these walks I raised the subject of Christian literature available in Tamil; for instance, I asked Lincoln whether there was a concordance to the Tamil Bible. He replied: "No David, the Tamil church has no concordance; in fact, there is a dearth of Tamil Christian literature of all kinds." I was staggered by this revelation and felt a strong urge to do something about it. The matter, however, gradually faded from my mind.

At the end of June I returned to Madras and my daily Tamil lesson in preparation for the second examination in November. I also resumed the task of leading the prayer meeting in the villages and one evening in September, on my way back from a meeting at Koyembedu, the boomerang hit me. The challenge I had met on the Kollis in June returned with even greater force. I had more or less vowed to undertake the task of compiling a concordance to the Tamil Bible but later forgotten all about it. During that twenty-minute cycle ride the Lord reminded me of that decision made three months earlier; now the project of such involvement seemed a frightening one and I demurred: "Lord, thousands of your servants have laboured in Tamilnadu, most of them better equipped than I, yet none of them prepared a Tamil Bible Concordance; so I certainly am not fit for such a task." The rejoinder was quick and stern: "The failure of others to produce a concordance is the very reason why you must do it."

With trepidation and at first complete secrecy I began the work, and twenty long years were to elapse before anything was to come of my efforts in this connection.

My second and final obligatory examination came up that November. As usual the written tests came first and the oral ordeal a week later. At the latter I had, among other things, to converse in Tamil with the three examiners and give a short address on a scripture passage, after half an hour's preparation. Thanks to my practical work at the village prayer meetings, my oral marks showed a great improvement over those of my first examination; in fact, by the Lord's goodness I secured distinction in the written and oral tests.

After a short break, Mr Booth gave me the responsibility of supervising the educational and evangelistic work in the rural area to the west of the City. We had our first meal of the day, known as "chota hazri", at 6.30 am prompt, after which I cycled to one of the villages for street preaching and colportage, that is book-selling, with a Tamil colleague. We usually had a fair audience before the men went to work. Later in the morning I often visited one or more schools and examined the pupils in Bible stories, Christian lyrics and catechism of scripture knowledge. Sometimes, however, desk work demanded an early return to the bungalow. At 11 am came "breakfast", after which the temperature usually kept us indoors; this was the time for correspondence, book-keeping and siesta. Tea was served at 2.30 pm, leaving the afternoon and early evening free for a variety of items; there were schools to visit, prayer meetings to conduct, deacons' meetings and magic lantern shows.

One of my duties was to write articles for the Mission Herald. In this connection I once got into trouble by quoting from a modern version of the Bible that was offensive to some of our readers. My ineptitude caused such a furore in Britain that I feared I might be thrown out of the Mission. However, the storm eventually blew over. Later, when I was in England on furlough, I had a conversation with one of our supporters whom I did not know. While we chatted I became curious as to his identity and asked him his name. As soon as he told me I realised that he was one of those who took objection to that article of mine. The Lord had evidently repaired the damage done at that time.

In the summer of 1924, in accordance with the Mission's regulations, I informed Council of my desire to get married at the end of the year. The rule was that a man missionary could marry after three years on foreign soil providing he had passed the second Tamil examination and that his fiancee was approved by Council. Although my request was completely in order, Council felt unable to give their consent; I was informed that the Mission did not need another married missionary at that time. Therefore I could apply again in a year's time. In the meantime, on her own initiative, Marty had taken the usual missionary training course for ladies. Moreover, being a trained and experienced midwife, she had contacted a woman who was shortly leaving for India with a baby a few weeks old. It was arranged that she should travel with this passenger and care for her and her infant during the voyage. Marty's steamer ticket had already been purchased; when she reached India she could live with her brother Lincoln and his family and

start Tamil study. But Council was adamant and the young
couple had to wait the fourth year. So I applied to Council
again in the middle of 1925. This time my request was
granted.

To the Tamils a bachelor is a bald-headed youth; when
he gets married his bare pate is exchanged for a crowned
one. I was given my crown at the Tamil Baptist Chapel in
Sendamangalam on 22 December 1925. It was a very quiet
wedding yet not without an exciting few moments. After
supper we sat in the garden and enjoyed a few fireworks.
One rocket which failed to extinguish itself landed on the
white silk dress of the chief bridesmaid, a missionary
colleague, Nellie Putnam! One gallant friend sprang to his
feet and put the fire out by giving Nellie's tummy a vigorous
rub! We had no honeymoon; immediately after Christmas,
Marty and I were posted to Madras to assist Mr and Mrs
Booth. I therefore, left Sendamangalam and went to the
City to find a place for us to live. With the help of friends I
soon secured a small house about half a mile from the
Mission bungalow.

I was happy to be back with my friends in the Madras
churches, and it was a joy to introduce Marty to the women
and girls of the various groups. She took regular Tamil
lessons and began to prepare for the first examination in
November 1926. However, ere long our nest was stirred up
once more. Although brother Booth bravely soldiered on
after partially recovering from another breakdown in
health, it soon became apparent that he would have to retire
as soon as possible. Consequently Lincoln and Ethel were
transferred from Sendamangalam to Madras early in the
year while the young Throwers took their place at
Sendamangalam; an upheaval which came just ten weeks
after we moved into our first home as a married couple.
There were no lorries to hire for the transport of our
belongings. Much hard labour was involved in wrapping

articles of furniture in wisps of straw, before being sent to
Salem by goods train and thence by bullock-cart to
Sendamangalam.

The Sendamangalam area was not new to me; I quickly
settled in to the camping routine, being away from home
three weekends each month. I also frequently preached at
an enormous weekly market held five miles away on
Wednesdays. Generally speaking Marty had to stay at home
and continue her language study. Her change of teacher
was a distinct disadvantage for her as each munshi (Indian
language teacher) had his own way of doing the job.

We made several tenting camps for evangelistic outreach
in many villages rarely if ever contacted with the Gospel in
any other way. A number of preachers and a colporteur
accompanied us, and large numbers of gospel portions were
sold. Marty took special leave from her munshi and came
on such camps. For one ten-day camp we were able to rent a
Government Travellers' Bungalow in the centre of a
populous area. Twenty-six villages and hamlets were
visited; in several of them evening meetings were held in the
main street of the place, the message being illustrated by
magic lantern slides. On one occasion we visited and
preached in many villages far from any road, and during the
camp several snakes were killed near the tents but, by God's
mercy, no one was bitten.

A week before Christmas, when Marty and I had been
married almost exactly a year, our first child was born.
Having delivered more than four hundred babies as a
midwife, Marty was quite happy to remain in
Sendamangalam for her confinement. Nellie Putnam kindly
offered to assist her and we also booked the doctor at the
local Government Hospital, just in case. In the event the
birth was an alarmingly difficult one; in fact it appeared to
have almost all the complications that could arise in the
case of a normal woman. By God's mercy and the

extraordinary resourcefulness shown by the doctor, Marty's life was spared, though the operation left her very weak for some time. The Lord who had given her, in His perfect wisdom and love took her back on Christmas Eve. "Little Olive" is still a precious member of our family; her death and burial in Tamilnadu became one of the great blessings of our career. The experience was, of course, a terrible one at the time, and I cannot say that we reacted with thankful hearts, but our Master's blessing followed and sweetened its memory in such a way that both Marty and I did later thank Him for giving us this particular key to comfort bereaved hearts. During the former part of our career, infant mortality was extremely high in Tamilnadu and I conducted many funerals. But our Lord gave us an experience of Himself as "The God of all comfort", that enabled us to lay a hand on a sorrowing parent's shoulder and say: "Brother and sister! We have walked this way and can sympathize with you; He who comforted us will console your stricken hearts."

Many years later I spoke at a special meeting for Christians in one of the Madras city churches. When the programme was finished I seem to have been in a hurry to get home. However, before I reached my vehicle I heard someone running after me and calling out. I stopped and found that it was a woman chasing me. When I asked her what she wanted she said something like this: "Mr Thrower! I want to tell you something. I and my family now live here in Madras but we formerly belonged to Namakkal. There, ten years ago, we lost our little boy. You were there at that time and you and Mrs Thrower visited us; your words have been a great comfort to us ever since. You told us of your own similar bereavement and how God comforted you."

We were only in Sendamangalam eighteen months; by September 1927 we returned to the metropolis of Madras.

The transfer was unexpected and came at a most inopportune time for us, for we had planned a two-week camp for gospel outreach in the far south of the area. In fact, we had actually embarked on this when a telegram arrived requesting us to pack our bags and leave for the city as soon as possible. Two bullock-carts loaded to capacity had set out for the camp site half an hour before the message reached us. I jumped on my motor-cycle and found the bandies (country carts) a mile and a half along the road. Sadly breaking the news to the drivers who were happily jogging along at their customary two and a half miles an hour, I told them to return immediately. On my return I endeavoured, with Marty's invaluable help, to sort out all that this shock would mean for us in the immediate future. Somehow we managed to get away a few days later, Marty by train from Salem and I with the motor-cycle and sidecar combination, which contained numerous "items" including our dog. Unfortunatly I had been so fully occupied during the preceding weeks that I had failed to pay proper attention to the state of my tyres. As a result I had such trouble on this journey; there were several punctures and a burst tyre. To my chagrin I finally turned up at the Mission house in Kilpauk half an hour later than David Morling and Jesse Brand who had left the Salem area two days after me! The latter had a good laugh at my expense.

Then we settled down to the routine work of the city that we knew so well. For the first few months we assisted Lincoln and Ethel in educational, evangelistic and church activities. Then they left for their second furlough early in 1928, after which we assumed full responsibility for all the varied activities that we took part in. While I was engaged in my many-sided ministry among the churches, Marty took care of Ethel's young women's sewing class, supervised the work of the Bible-women, (Christian women who were employed to visit Indian homes and teach Scripture to the womenfolk) and also took and passed the second Tamil examination in May of that year.

During our summer vacation Marty and I had the privilege of initiating a rapprochement between the Strict Baptist Mission and the South Indian Strict Baptist Missionary Society which led to the amalgamation of these two bodies the following year. Both represented Strict Baptist Churches in Britain and functioned separately since 1895, when unhappily a split occurred. In May 1928 I felt an urge to do something towards healing the rift. At that time South Indian Strict Baptist Missionary Society had only two single ladies on the Indian staff, whilst the Strict Baptist Mission had ten missionaries. Marty and I met the ladies of the South Indian Mission, at Ootacamund while we were all there on holiday: we spent a day out together on a picnic and gave a good deal of the time to prayer regarding the possibility of the amalgamation of our Mission. Our desire to see the rift healed was shared with our SBM colleagues and in due course a letter was sent to the home boards of both Missions appealing to them to combine forces. Our appeal received sympathetic consideration by both bodies, with the result that the SBM Council and the SISBMS. Committees met on 2 August 1929 and unanimously passed resolutions for the amalgamation of their missionary societies. As a result the Annual Meetings of the SBM included an amalgamation Thanksgiving service.

1928 was my seventh year in South India and Council decided that we should take our first furlough the following year. On our return to Tamilnadu early in 1930, we were to relieve the Brands on the Kolli Hills, so that they could leave for a long overdue furlough. With this in view and at the invitation of the Brands I spent two weeks seeing something of their work in various parts of the Kolli Hills towards the end of 1926. This visit was to prove of great value to Marty and me for a reason unknown to us at that time.

At the beginning of 1929 Lincoln and Ethel returned from furlough and we proceeded to Britain. Our voyage was a restful uneventful trip as far as Port Said. But as soon as we entered the Mediterranean we ran into increasingly unpleasant weather. We encountered high winds and a choppy sea that became really rough as we approached the area lying to the south of the Adriatic Sea. The "Merkara" was due to call at Malta, but that was nearly a thousand miles from Port Said. By the third day, which was a Sunday, the "Merkara" rolled like a tub as she was battered by a fierce storm blowing southward from the Alps. I conducted a morning service in the dining saloon, but the congregation was a small one, no doubt partly due to the weather conditions. As our course lay from east to west the northerly wind beat more and more menacingly on our starboard beam as the day wore on. The comparatively small vessel was tossed about like a toy in the gale which reached the strength of eighty miles an hour throughout that never-to-be-forgotten Lord's Day. By the afternoon the ship seemed to be on her beam ends at every lurch; nothing aboard stayed in place unless tethered. It was impossible to stand without holding on to a rail. Every wave swept the decks and one went right over the ship.

The movement aboard was such that passengers' trunks cannonaded against the walls of their cabins. One lady thought she could escape being hurled about by taking refuge on her bunk, an upper one! She soon found herself on the floor! It was an alarming experience; but the Captain thoughtfully sent an officer to assure the passengers that they were in no danger. There was no panic; indeed, the passengers remained commendably calm. Once the deck appeared to drop from under our feet as the "Merkara" slithered to the bottom of the trough of an enormous wave.

Another wave that filled the decks sucked open a door with a faulty latch. We saw the water come through that door and rush down two flights of stairs into the dining saloon; it was not a pleasant sight! At dinnertime that evening only one intrepid passenger managed to reach a table in the saloon. A steward repeatedly tried to serve the man with dinner, but the bucking vessel scuppered both him and the soup he was carrying; it was impossible. Now our problem; Marty was seven months pregnant. Some passengers, including ourselves, thought the safest place under the circumstances was in one of the companion ways where we could hold a hand-rail. In the later evening the skipper took the precautions of reducing speed and steering the ship into the wind. After that we pitched and tossed instead of rolling. This was very helpful for us passengers and we spent a reasonably comfortable night, and by our Heavenly Father's protection, Marty sustained no injury. The storm blew itself out before morning; when we got up the sea was perfectly calm.

We entered Valetta harbour, Malta that Monday morning and were able to go ashore for an hour or two. It was delightful to walk on solid ground once more. Our feelings were fittingly expressed by the phrase "terra firma" which we interpreted as – the more the firmer, the less the terror!

In the late spring the half-yearly meetings of the Mission was held at St John's Wood Baptist Church, constituting, among other things, our official welcome. There was an afternoon devotional gathering, tea and a large evening rally. The evening meeting had a long programme, on which my name was the last. As various persons took a share in the proceedings they all seemed to repeat the refrain: "I know you are eagerly waiting to hear the missionary, so I won't take up much time". In this way the former parts of the programme was telescoped into a very

short space of time and I was left with well over an hour at
my disposal. I don't remember how I utilised the time apart
from one item. I sang a Tamil lyric.

Our elder son, Vivian John, was born early in April at
Marty's home in Clapham. A few days later I had to leave
my wife and infant; nine days ministry, including the two
Sundays, called me to Suffolk. In addition to conducting
services on the Sundays, I cycled to a different village for a
meeting almost every evening. One day I went to a church
ten miles or more away in a blizzard. However, in spite of
this and other minor difficulties, it was a blessed time of
service and fellowship. The furlough was a normal one until
the latter part of June; but after that our further stay in
Britain became the subject of serious doubt as a result of
tragic news from Tamilnadu.

On 18 June we learned that our colleague Jesse Brand
had died three days earlier after a short illness. On Sunday
9 June he preached in the Valavanthi church although he
had fever. On the Tuesday he took to bed with a severe
attack of malignant malaria. Blackwater fever quickly
developed and on Saturday 15 he went to his Lord. This
was a staggering blow for Marty and me as we faced the
task of following our brother in the work on the Kollis. In
the meantime, however, I had the daunting prospect of
having to speak at Evelyn Brand's home church on the
evening of that very day. For an hour or two I felt quite
unable to face it and foolishly hoped the meetings might be
postponed. However, after a while, I pulled myself together
and sought divine help to fulfil the engagement. Then,
hardly knowing what to say, I gave some sort of address on
Joshua 1:2: "My servant is dead; now therefore arise; go
over . . ." Miss Ruth Harris a niece of Mrs Brand, was in
the congregation. She later testified that the meeting held at
the church three days after her uncle Jesse's homecall
played its part in her desire for missionary service in

Tamilnadu. A few years later, as Dr Ruth Harris, she commenced a medical ministry among the Tamils that she continued for about forty years.

Marty and I suggested that we return to India at once, but Council felt that we needed a full nine months furlough after a seven-year period of hard work. So we continued our deputation duties a few months longer. During that time, I spent a week with friends at Rushden, not far from Bedford. From there we paid never-to-be-forgotten visits to such Bunyan landmarks as Bedford, Elstow and Carlton, for ministry and sight-seeing. Ere long, however, we learned that Mrs Brand was not happy to leave the Kollis until someone was available to care for the work. It was, therefore, decided that Marty and I should return to Tamilnadu in the autumn.

We were stationed on the Kolli Hills for slightly less than three years. This range of mountains apparently got its name, which literally means the Killer Hills, from the malignant type of malaria for which it is notorious. There was church work, outreach by street preaching in the villages and the supervision of eight elementary schools and a girls' hostel. The medical ministry was cared for by an Indian Christian doctor. The many industries included the felling of trees for timber, making and burning bricks, a carpentry school and various forms of agriculture. Regular weekend camps on all but the first weekend of each month was the order here as on the plains. But my mode of travel was very different from what I had been used to. I soon became accustomed to using Jesse Brand's horse; an ideal type of transport on the rough terrain of the Kollis. A feature of the Christian community on the Kolli Hills that was different from conditions prevailing in other areas of the Mission's work was the settlement at Valavanthi; all the Kolli Hills Christians lived there, having become outcasts by their conversion and therefore unable to continue to live in their villages.

A kind friend, wishing to protect Marty, Vivian and me from the attentions of the malarial mosquitoes, generously sent us a large roll of mosquito-proof copper wire mesh. This our carpenter fixed to all windows and verandahs, whilst doors were fitted with springs. After this work was completed we were reasonably safe from infection, at least while we were in the bungalow. On camp I used a mosquito net at night but repeatedly developed fever after camps in spite of this precaution but with one exception the rest of the family escaped malarial infection. The exception occurred when Marty undertook two midwifery cases on consecutive nights and caught a double infection. Our doctor sometimes had dreadful cases of bear mauling to treat. These beasts were very numerous in the hill jungles; in fact one was once seen from the Mission house in broad daylight.

In March 1931 the Lord gave us our second son Irwin Jesse.

It was my earliest intention and desire to erect a headstone at the grave of our esteemed colleague, Jesse Brand, at Valavanthi. But this constituted a difficult project from several points of view, particularly in the matter of transport. First we had to locate a rock from which a suitable piece could be taken. After considerable effort we succeeded in finding such a rock about a quarter of a mile from the grave. We lit a fire on the rock and heated it until it cracked. This operation was successfully accomplished, after which we started to transport the stone to the site. Half a dozen stout rollers were cut from a straight tree trunk – strong rope and two crowbars were used by a team of thirty two men for this and after three and a half days of prodigious toil, the stone had been dragged down a hill, across a flooded rice field and finally for some distance uphill to the grave. There a stone-mason rounded the top, smoothed the surfaces and chipped out a cavity to take an inscribed memorial tablet of marble. At last this memorial to our brother's life and ministry was erected in it's rightful place; mission successfully accomplished.

Another piece of work attended to, was the construction of a school building near the village of Chulavanthi in the southern part of the plateau. Bricks were made and burnt in a kiln near the site and trees purchased to provide timber for doors, windows and roof. Then the question arose: "When should we take a gang of workmen and women from Valavanthi and erect the building?" This constituted an important question; great inconvenience and loss could ensue in the event of tropical rain falling while such work was in progress, so we chose the month of February, when the Kollis "never" have rain. But we were mistaken. As soon as the walls were up and we were ready to put the roof on, torrential downpours overtook us on two consecutive days. We had our two small sons with us under canvas and the rain caught us so suddenly that the tent threatened to collapse on us. With heavy hearts we returned to headquarters on the third day and the building had to be completed later.

Later on, Marty's health and mine began to give way under the strain of malignant malaria, following an abnormally long term in Tamilnadu and a very short furlough. In fact Marty suffered a complete breakdown early in 1932, my health being not a great deal better. Owing to our impaired health Marty and I were given double the normal vacation period that summer. While this was very helpful, both of us were far from fit when we returned to the Kollis. Upon seeing our condition, two of our colleagues suggested the postponement of their own furlough, due at the end of the year, so that Marty and I could proceed to Britain as soon as practicable. We were profoundly thankful for this gesture which undoubtedly saved our health and missionary career.

A couple of weeks after our arrival in London Marty and
I were examined by the Mission's medical officer. He
reported that there was nothing organically wrong with
either of us but that both of us were suffering from nervous
exhaustion and needed six months to recuperate. He asked
us to leave our children in the care of relatives and spend
two months at Bournemouth followed by a month at
Brighton. After that we were to see him again. As it was
already the end of November the doctor agreed to our
postponing our seaside holiday until after Christmas. The
three months' rest and change proved extremely helpful
especially to Marty. At first she could hardly walk at all but
by the end of the time was able to enjoy two or three hours
walk a day. But her mother did not have such a successful
time looking after Vivian and Irwin in London.
Communication presented a major problem; when she
spoke to the boys they replied to her in Tamil! Poor mother
became very frustrated by this language issue but gallantly
bore the burden for those three months.

Early in April we returned to London greatly refreshed
and visited the Mission doctor again as instructed. He was
very pleased with the improvement in our health. In fact he
was so satisfied with my condition that he declared me fit to
undertake   normal   deputation   work   immediately.
Furthermore, I could return to India at the end of the year.
Marty, however, would need to spend an additional six
months in Britain, until the middle of 1934.

When on furlough I was not altogether out of my Tamil
"element", for writing and translation work usually
occupied part of my time. Literature tasks that had to be
kept going at least had the merit of preventing my Tamil
from becoming rusty. Throughout this furlough I continued
translating daily Bible study notes which I did for a number
of years at that period. Another item in this category at
that time was the checking of material produced by

my co-worker L Benjamin in the compilation of the Concordance to the Tamil Bible.

As the furlough approached its close towards the end of the year, I was able to praise the Lord for His goodness towards us, especially in the realm of our health. So without waiting for Christmas I left for India at the beginning of December. Marty and the boys remained in the flat at Clapham. The parting was not a pleasant experience for any of us, but God gave us all needed grace and enabled us to take it in our stride. After a good voyage I landed at Bombay on my wedding anniversary just before Christmas and proceeded to Madras by train. At a meeting of our Indian co-workers to welcome me back, Lincoln read the telegram I had sent from Bombay. It read "arriving Express Saturday evening Second Epistle John twelve."

Someone found and read out the reference! "Having many things to write to you, I would not write with paper or ink; but I trust to come to you and speak face to face that our joy may be full."

The Strict Baptist Mission was formed in 1861 out of a concern to maintain the Calvinistic distinctives which had spurred on Carey. Work was concentrated in the Tamil-speaking areas around Madras. For thirty-five years the work was carried on by paid agents under the supervision of English Christians already resident in India. The first missionaries, Samuel Hutchinson and Ernest Booth, arrived in this region in 1895. Despite discouragements and divisions by the goodness of God the work gradually expanded.

Mission work in India at this time was part of a paternalistic system in which Indians were treated as second-class citizens. Although inevitably a part of this system, from the beginning of his time in India David began to use every opportunity to build up mutual confidence and to enable the Indian churches to become self-governing. One such opportunity was the Throwers' "experiment" (as David described it) to free a group of Christian believers from the grip of debt-collectors by forming a loan association. Over the years David involved himself in a number of practical projects such as brick-making, the improvement of paths and tracks, and even the construction of a sun-dial.

Coupled with this enterprising spirit – David was always willing to try something new if it furthered the gospel – there was a childlike simplicity. For a time during this period David and Marty became convinced that God wanted them to live "by faith" as a test of their obedience to Him. And so live "by faith" they did.

3.
By all means

Having arrived in Madras just before Christmas 1933 I had the pleasure of conducting the Christmas service at the Kilpauk Church. A few days later I took leave of Lincoln and Ethel and went to Namakkal, which was to be my sphere of work until the Spring of the following year.

Namakkal town is situated at the foot of a round rock-hill three hundred feet high; its chief Hindu temple is dedicated to Hanuman, the monkey god. It is an ideal centre for evangelistic outreach, having seven roads radiating from it to all parts of the taluk, (an administrative area, like an English county,) so I regularly camped at weekends at most of the suitable places. Nearly all of those on my side of the taluk were situated on or near the bank of the Cauvery river about twenty miles to the west of Namakkal. There were six or seven village churches and schools, whilst the largest group of believers was in the village of Sirunellikoil, two miles from the river. I frequently preached in the chapel there although the place was somewhat difficult to reach as it was two miles from a road.

When not visiting the villages I had plenty to do in headquarters, for the Namakkal church had two services on Sundays and a mid-week prayer meeting. I also conducted Bible classes for senior and junior boys in the hostel and monthly Bible classes for our Indian co-workers. There was also of course, outreach to the Hindus around us by preaching and literature distribution.

51

Marty, Vivian and Irwin returned to India in October and I met them at Madras Harbour. It was the first time any of us had landed at this port, a very gracious provision by the Lord, as it saved Marty the strain of a long train journey with our small sons. I waited on the quay and watched the ship pull alongside. Looking up at the passengers on the deck I soon spotted the five year old Vivian standing on the railings at the edge of the deck. I was scared lest the little chap should slip and fall into the water below! And so our little family was again united, after nearly a year.

Three days later we left Madras by the night train and completed the journey to Namakkal by bus early the next morning. Marty took over the house-keeping and soon put the house in order, and I was very happy to see that her health had been fully restored. In fact, she was able a few weeks later to bring the children and accompany me on a two-weeks' camp.

After proceeding as far as we could by bus, we sent the camping equipment to Sirunellikoil by bullock-cart while we walked the two miles in the cool of the evening. I frequently gave the boys pick-a-back rides and we reached the village and chapel before dark. The bullock-cart had arrived, so we unpacked our gear and began to settle in. All had gone well so far, except that I appeared to have lost a five rupee note during the work. I was quite upset by this mishap and my five-year-old elder son heard me moaning about it. He said: "Don't worry, Daddy; Jesus can send the money down from heaven." We all knelt on the mud floor and committed the matter to Him. A day or two later the local pastor and I decided to spend two or three days visiting a number of villages several miles away, travelling by springless bullock-cark and camping in school buildings. Marty packed my bedding in a holdall that had been kept on one of the beams supporting the chapel roof. As soon as

she moved the holdall something from under it fluttered to
the floor – the missing five rupee note. We once more knelt
on the floor, this time to thank Jesus for sending the note
down to us. Our young son's faith had been rewarded; his
father was taught a much-needed lesson.

As we wended our way back in the evening dusk we had
to walk single file through a dense mass of ten feet high
prickly pear cactus. There I trod on a snake without
noticing it. But the pastor following me saw it and observed
that I placed my foot so that the creature became wedged
between the sole and heel of my shoe. It was unable to
strike, for its head was buried in the cactus on one side of
the path while its tail was in the bushes on the other side. It
was apparently uninjured and, when I lifted my foot,
proceeded on its way. The reptile was probably a cobra, for
that kind of snake it very partial to prickly pear; in fact the
Tamil name for that cactus literally means, "The cobra's
marriage symbol." The incident reminded us of the
scripture promise of Psalm 91: "You will tread upon the . . .
cobra".

Many varieties of snakes abound in Tamilnadu; we have
from time to time encountered these reptiles. On one
occasion I went through a partly open door of the house in
Kilpauk and was startled by a snake that fell on my head
from the top of the door; from where it slipped to the floor
and scuttled away, probably as frightened as I was. On
another occasion some men chased a snake six feet or more
in length in the garden of the Mission house. In its attempt
to escape it crawled along a verandah of the building.
Vivian ran to the door of the verandah to see what was
happening; his father quickly followed him. Father and son
stood in the doorway, the latter on a step leading down to
the verandah. The snake rapidly approached the step and I
was only just in time to lift Vivian up, the snake passing
under him. We had many escapades with cobras, rat snakes

and vipers. One rat snake that I killed a few yards from "Danvi", Kotagiri was about ten feet long!

About that time I began to receive requests to speak at special meetings or to give a series of addresses during a weekend. These calls came from Tamil church leaders almost all over Tamilnadu. One weekend in October 1934 I ministered to several groups connected with the London Missionary Society in Salem and a few months later was invited to visit them again. On this second visit one of my addresses was to a young people's class, the subject being, by request, "Why I teach believers' baptism and what it means." Another evening I attended a function at which the congregation bade farewell to a missionary couple who had served them for thirty-five years. Before the meeting I was told that the friend who was retiring was very fond of children and never failed to greet them when preaching. But he also never failed to amuse the adults by a small error in his pronunciation of the word for "children". He invariably addressed his young friends as "my dear tigers". I therefore listened for the big game in his response to the farewell message; sure enough, out it came! What a warning for the visiting speaker!

Such small errors sometimes cause not amusement but acute embarrassment. Therefore soon after I began to speak in Tamil I formed the habit of seeking help from my congregation. I gave a notebook and pencil to the most intelligent looking person present, requesting them to help the foreigner by noting every error, whether of pronunciation, grammar, diction, idiom, etc., and the practice proved most valuable.

In February 1935 we left Namakkal on transfer to Madras, where we quickly settled in to the well-known work in the City and its environs. It was then that Stanley Jones the well known preacher and writer who earlier spent many years in North India visited Madras. It was arranged for

him to speak at a mass meeting of Christians in a cinema.
The reception committee asked me to translate for him; I
therefore saw him the previous day regarding the subject of
his address. But I need not have taken that trouble as, in the
event, the Doctor changed much of his matter and spoke in
a free, extemporaneous manner. Every seat in the building
was occupied before it commenced, and after a brief prayer
Dr Jones was introduced. Not a moment was lost by either
of us for the next hour and a half, as we considered the
subject, "Why I believe in the resurrection of Jesus Christ."
The speech was a clear and scriptural statement of the
message of Easter.

The calls that I received for the ministry of the Word in
various parts of Tamilnadu included two with rarely
experienced openings for outreach to largely non-Christian
audiences. One of these was at Chingleput, a District
headquarters town not far from Madras. In addition to
several meetings in the Christian church, arrangements
were for me to speak at an evening meeting in the Public
Reading Room, where a lawyer living in the town was asked
to take the chair. A large majority of those present were
non-Christians. My subject was "The New Birth". The
other such meeting was at Tiruvannamalai, a taluk headquarters' town where I spoke several times in a Christian
Secondary School and preached at the Church on a Sunday
morning. As at Chingleput arrangements had been made
for me to address a gathering in the Public Reading Room
that Sunday evening. On this occasion my chairman was a
local member of the Madras State Parliament, the
Legislative Assembly. Nearly all those present were middle-
class men of the town, such as shop-keepers, and teachers.
Most of them were completely topless apart from the usual
multi-purpose length of cloth thrown over the left shoulder.
The topic I chose for this occasion was "The Light of the
World", chosen because the Hindu festival of Light would

shortly be celebrated through Tamilnadu, having its centre
in that town. On that day a half a million people would
gather from far and near for the great function.

Another piece of special ministry that I had the privilege
of rendering at this period was that of preaching at the
Graduation Service at a theological college in Vellore.
Taking the first half of Phil. 3:20 as my text, "Our
citizenship in heaven" I drew the attention of the new
graduates to four different renderings of this statement in
the Tamil versions of the New Testament. These roughly
agreed with the English translations – our conversation,
commonwealth, citizenship . . .is in heaven. I pointed out
that they had only just begun to study the scriptures; they
must spend the rest of their lives studying to show themselves faithful and efficient exponents of the Word of God.

On Hindu, Muslim and Christian festival days, when
schools, banks, business houses and factories were closed, a
goodly number of our Tamil brethren from the churches of
the area teamed up and made a special effort to reach as
many people as possible with the Gospel. They selected
specially needy parts of our area or even beyond the borders
within which we normally operated. There they engaged in
street preaching and colportage. Also in Madras there was a
number of young men keen to engage in church planting
and nurturing in the outlying areas. At first they went
individually by cycle to one of the smaller worshipping
groups and assisted the local workers at Sunday services.
Then they joined forces and at Mannur, a few miles west of
Madras an opportunity came to begin regular gospel
witness. After a while they noticed an unused chapel
building and utilized it as a base for their work, faithfully
carrying on until the Mannur Tamil Baptist Church was
formed. Today that church is one of the most vigorous
centres of Christian witness in our Madras area, and the
pastor is a local man.

The four main churches of the area – Ayanapuram, Poonamalee, Sembiam and Vepery – functioned as fully organised bodies, but only the last two had indigenously appointed Tamil pastors. The other two churches and their outlying groups of members were, therefore, still under the direction of the local missionary. Consequently, first Lincoln, and later I trained the various groups of believers to develop indigenous life, initiative and control in their church affairs. But until they were able to appoint their own pastors I served as chairman, but not controller, of deacons' meetings, and church business meetings. All in all, however, the churches demanded a great deal of my time and energy.

The churches had a total membership of three hundred and thirty two, twenty-five persons being baptized that year after public profession of faith in the Lord Jesus Christ. Such statistics do not, of course, prove spiritual progress in individuals or churches. But regular instruction in the Word of God in two services on Sunday, prayer meetings and pastoral visitations must have borne fruit; the assessment thereof must be left to our Lord. In addition the Mission in Madras was responsible for thirteen elementary day schools and twenty-one Sunday Schools with a total strength of nearly a thousand pupils. The children learned scripture narratives, Gospel lyrics and a simple catechism dealing with fundamental truths.

The compilation of the Tamil Bible Concordance went ahead slowly but efficiently through the faithful and skilled labours of brother Benjamin. Although the work was not far enough advanced to start printing, the Superintendent of Christian Literature Society, Madras, was keen to stir up interest in this essential book of reference for Christian workers. He, therefore, had a number of specimen pages printed and distributed to Christian leaders throughout Tamilnadu. It was obviously good for a certain amount of prayerful interest in this project to be elicited in this way.

My work in literature continued, and a small but specialized task came to hand, – the translation of a pamphlet on "Forgiveness of Sin" into Tamil for those working among Muslims. This involved the replacement of all religious terms normally used in Tamil by their Urdu equivalents; for the followers of Islam do not know the Tamil words for such things as prayer and forgiveness and sin. As my facility for the Tamil language grew, so more jobs came my way.

It was my privilege to serve on the missionaries' United Language Examination Board and panel of Tamil examiners for some years. The work of the Board was well organised, for twelve examiners were involved in each examination, preparing written papers, allotting marks to the candidates, and conducting oral tests. Much hard work and considerable responsibility were involved. For instance, the oral part of the examinations sometimes required two full days' work. Also, towards the end of 1935 I was requested to take charge of the Tamil language school for missionaries, the man then running it being about to leave India. I gladly took on this honorary task which did not demand a great deal of my time and energy, while involving me in educational work. The school had two experienced pundits and about a dozen missionary students representing a variety of Missions.

During the year, we began to feel the need for a larger vehicle than the motor-cycle and side-car combination that we were using, but could not afford a car. It appeared that a Raleigh three-wheel delivery van could be within our means and solve the problem. As the Raleigh Company had no agency in this country we purchased one of these vehicles from London. The van arrived in Madras in May where we succeeded in converting it into a five-seater that became well known in Madras and many other places in

Tamilnadu; it appears to have been the only vehicle of its kind in India. I then set out to teach a number of people to drive, using our Raleigh trike. My first pupil in this school was Marty who passed her test the first time round in spite of being taken for a very difficult trial run by the Test Inspector. One of my pupils, Sagayam was not so successful. The inspector got into the Raleigh, Sagayam at the wheel. I was permitted to occupy a rear seat. Off we went; a few yards along the road Sagayam made straight for a jutka, a pony-cart. The inspector grabbed the hand-brake! A little further on our budding driver tried to charge into the middle of another vehicle, at which the inspector gave appropriate advice to Sagayam, got out and walked back to his office!

In March 1939 Marty and I, with our three children, left for furlough. However, a month before we were due to sail, our daughter Olive, three years old, developed what was diagnosed as diptheria. This seriously threatened to postpone our travel. The doctor who treated Olive had herself lost a child of about Olive's age through that disease; she therefore exercised the utmost care in dealing with our little one's case. By God's goodness Olive rapidly recovered and the doctor assured us that there was no need for us to delay our departure. The only proviso was that Olive must not be allowed to walk for the first three weeks on board. In the event this presented no problem as Vivian, a ten-year old, carried his little sister about all the three weeks and completely relieved Marty and me of the task.

Less than one week before we left Madras we had the sad duty of conducting the funeral of Preacher Devamanickam, an esteemed Tamil Colleague. He had for many years been stationed in the village of Kolathur where, in spite of much persecution, he courageously laboured for the Lord until pulmonary tuberculosis ended his career. He and I spent many happy hours preaching in villlages in the Kolathur area as well as in the school building where we held Sunday afternoon services and mid-week prayer meetings for the Kolathur group of believers. One of the outstanding victories of my time in Tamilnadu was won when I felt a strong urge to tackle brother Devamanickam's three arch-enemies in the village. It took hours of dogged persistent refusing to give up the spiritual fight until it was won. For the praise of God alone, I am able to say that none of them persecuted him after that encounter one Sunday. I also visited him many times during his final illness, the last occasion being a few hours before his Lord took him home to Himself. He was fully conscious, recognised me and assured me of his complete trust in the Lord Jesus Christ and his readiness to go to Him. Shortly after my visit he told his relatives to roll up the bedding, as he was going on a journey and would not need it where he was going.

The event that marked that furlough more than anything else, was, of course, the outbreak of World War Two in September 1939.

As soon as war was declared all children were evacuated from London. Vivian and Irwin were due to return to school after their summer vacation. We therefore took Olive along with her brothers and put her into the school at Swansea early in September. She had just celebrated her fourth birthday, and she joined a happy group of kindergarten pupils under the care of a kind, experienced matron. Our furlough programme ended rather sadly with a memorial service for my old colleague Ernest Booth who had died earlier. It was through the words of Ernest Booth that I had received my call to overseas service eighteen years earlier, so it was good to be at this gathering.

So we set out to resume our work in Tamilnadu, wartime conditions notwithstanding. Our hearts were filled with gratitude to God for the remarkable provision made by Him for our children's care and education two hundred miles west of London although it was with great sadness and difficulty that we left them behind, especially our little Olive who was so small.

With the passing of 1939, the phoney war was replaced by Hitler's Germany sowing magnetic mines in the English Channel, which blew up ships passing over them. The Royal Navy swept the shipping lane clear for our steamer, and an aircraft, on the lookout for submarines, also accompanied the vessel until it left the Channel. Those were the early months of the war, before ships sailed in convoys. We also had a few wartime precautions to cope with, but we were, however, profoundly thankful that we had no real trouble, and reached our destination on schedule.

How good it was to be back on the job in Madras and we soon settled in to the accustomed routine.

For a long time Marty and I had been greatly distressed by the perpetual indebtedness of the poorer section of the Tamil Christian community, most of whom are in the hands of a notorious class of professional money-lenders. Thus, when a sum of £100 unexpectedly became available for our use during our recent furlough, we dedicated it to the task of relieving at least a few of our Lord's poor, from debt. Our Tamil believing friends had been delivered from their bondage to sin, but were still hobbling about, bound by the hold the money-lenders had over them.

Soon after reaching Madras, therefore, we began to tackle this problem in a small way. We started with the members of the Mission staff, the teachers and preachers, nearly all of whom were in debt. They had no idea of putting a little by for a rainy day; every birth, wedding, death or attack of ill-health had to be paid for by borrowing.

What did we do? Well, throughout the war years from February 1940 onwards, every person who applied to us for a loan was, in the first instance, given nothing but a serious piece of instruction from the Word of God. We told our

friends that they were profaning the holy name of their
heavenly Father by not asking Him to supply their needs,
but, instead of waiting for His provision or guidance, going
to one of His enemies to get what they needed. If the
applicant was a married man we then asked him to bring
his wife to see us. We then felt ready to go into the details of
the person's indebtedness. This took time, as our friends
were not very forth-coming regarding this subject! Finally,
if there appeared to be a genuine readiness to accept
complete reorientation towards money, I went with the
person to the money-lender and redeemed whatever had
been placed in pawn, jewellery perhaps, or a property
document. Then I arranged for repayment to me to be
made at a rate no higher than the rate that was due to be
paid to the pawnbroker as current interest; *only* one anna
per rupee borrowed, per month! Often double this amount
was extorted by unscrupulous money lenders. (an anna was
$1/16$ of a rupee). After dealing with our Tamil co-workers'
debts I occasionally tackled one of our other church
members regarding his or her financial situation. On one
occasion I had a talk with a deacon of one of the churches.
At first he assured me that he had a good job and there was
no need for him to get into debt. But when I probed deeper
my friend said, "I don't regard it as debt, but I have taken a
loan from a money-lender and given my wife's jewels as
security. You see sir, it was like this. We had a family of
girls and then God gave us the great joy of having a son. We
were so thankful that we decided to give our church a set of
silver communion-ware as a thankoffering. But how were
we to get the money for this? Well, we pawned my wife's
jewellery to raise the cash. There's nothing wrong with that,
is there?

I was then able to give the brother a little teaching from
the Scriptures concerning his action in putting God's money
into the money lender's pocket month by month. Finally we

went to the pawnbrokers, and, after I had settled the man's bill, I was handed a pair of earrings. These I kept in the safe in my office until he had cleared his account with me.

However much or little our people learned through the operation of our debt relief scheme, I certainly learned much regarding the life of the Tamil masses that I could not have come to know in any other way.

Later on in Madras we started another innovation which was to bring us much encouragement. This was an Easter morning service to which we invited members of all our churches in the area to join. Several hundred persons met in the shade of some large tamarind trees in the mission house compound. The first Easter Sunday service was such a success that this united gathering became an annual event for at least the next decade.

Marty held a sewing class at Kilpauk, and she was able to note, "Nine of the girls are members of one or other of the churches. Another has declared her faith and is a staunch believer in the Lord Jesus, although her guardian refuses to permit her to be baptised. Several others are very near the Kingdom. The Christians are not only saved, but also realise that they are saved to serve. Their love for the Bible and hymnbook has given them a keenness for reading so that their minds and lives have expanded with the years. Their desire for the salvation of kith and kin is often noticeable; 'I wonder if Amma (mother – a Tamil word used as a term of respect for a lady) could spare time to come and have a prayer meeting in our house?' or 'My mother is nervous of coming with me. If our teacher, Esther, could call for my mother I am sure she would come'.".

Also at this time, one of our senior missionaries became seriously ill and as a result various duties passed on to me. I was initially asked to take on the job of Field Treasurer, which was to prove not too demanding, but then I was requested to act as chairman of the Annual Mission

Conference that we all attended. These occasions were often most helpful times of fellowship and teaching ministry from God's Word, whilst they also served to strengthen and invigorate weakened bodies. I am no leader and have never pretended to be one, yet I managed to struggle through a number of these occasions with the Lord's help.

A little later, I was given a General Power of Attorney, signed by the Lord Mayor of London! I still hold that Power, and am called on to use it from time to time.

Later on that year I was able to record, that, "we have much cause for praise; but at the same time, long to see greater things. These are days of tremendous challenge and opportunity. May our God help us to be faithful to Him and to the commission He has entrusted to us, just like Caleb, who wholly followed the Lord".

After Pearl Harbour at the end of 1941, our eastern enemies overran one country after another in the Far East, and it soon looked as if India might be one of their main targets. Between 13th and 15th February 1942 Singapore fell, and panic took hold of Madras which was one of two ports on the east coast of India that were bombed. The families of service personnel were hurriedly sent away from there and tension mounted. A strict blackout was enforced at night, creating difficulties for the people owing to the tropical heat. Before the middle of April tens of thousands were leaving the metropolis daily, and our work was sometimes handicapped by military restrictions on the use of certain roads.

The Madras Government issued three communiques urging those whose business did not keep them in the city to move to some place at least one hundred miles from the east coast. The last of these warnings was much stronger than the earlier ones and instructed all whose presence was not essential to leave the city. Finally, on 14th April, all the women and children living in the Kilpauk mission compound left by train for Salem en route to Sendamangalam. There were tremendous crowds at the railway station but our folk, by the Lord's goodness, were able to board the train and reach their destination on time the next morning. Later the same day my clerk and I travelled in the trike which was heavily loaded with as many of our necessary goods as possible.

Then, on 22nd April, seven days after our arrival at Sendamangalam, my clerk and I set out on the return trip to Madras to spend a few days in the city, providing there was no invasion. Before our arrival at Kilpauk the governor of Madras notified the public that the threat from the enemy had disappeared. It was reported that an invasion armada actually set out from Singapore and headed for the Indian coast, but inexplicably changed course and went to Rangoon. What a relief! What cause for thankfulness! There was no further threat to the Indian coast.

At this period we spent a whole year on an experiement in 'living by faith'. We had met a number of Christian workers known as faith missionaries and learned of the financial embarrassment some of them experienced. This led Marty and me to think seriously about the subject, with the result that we decided to see how our theories worked in practice. We had always regarded ourselves as faith missionaries for, although we were provided with a regular stipend, the Council would not go into debt under any circumstances. In fact, on one occasion, they had to cut our salaries by more than 20% for a short time.

After much prayerful thought we felt that it could be helpful for us to look to the Lord still more directly for our support for a period of a year. Throughout that period, as soon as our salary was received, we set aside a small sum to spend on bread. The remainder we sent away month by month to some good cause. I wish to make it clear that we have never recommended anyone to follow our example in this, nor would we wish to do so. All we desired was to learn something about faith for the supply of our own needs. We decided to start with ten days on toasted bread and water, followed by the stores that we had in the house and thereafter spending nothing but our bread money from our regular income. But we would supplement our diet with whatever the Lord provided in other ways. One of the results was that plain toast became so sweet to us that even today it is immaterial to me whether it has anything on it or not. That year was the most amazing period of our lifetime, war conditions notwithstanding. It was a genuine test, for no one would in the ordinary course give anything to the Throwers for their support – they weren't faith missionaries. Yet in spite of this, we had some overwhelming experiences during that year, but never before or since.

Some time previously a Tamil friend had given us a small chicken to turn into soup; but Marty kept it and it grew into a hen. The day after we started our fast this pullet laid its first egg, and Marty and I had half an egg each on our toast for dinner. We also had a few goats and within a few days after the pullet's first egg, two of the goats produced kids and started to supply us with milk. A little later, while we were actually eating one of our frugal meals, the postman arrived with a Money Order. It was for thirty Rupees (about Rs13 to the £1) and it was from an Indian friend hundreds of miles away who had sent it with a note: "This represents a tithe of my income, for both my wife and I feel that God wishes us to send this amount to you each month. Please use it as He leads you". The money came from this couple every month for the next three years. A few weeks after the Money Orders episode a young single Tamil woman gave Marty another Thirty Rupees saying that God had told her to give it, a tenth of her salary. We were to use the money as God led us but say nothing about it to anyone.

And this person continued this practice every month till the end of the year. So the series of 'deliverances' went on. Gifts came by cheque, hard cash, and provisions.

Then a more severe test than we had bargained for overtook us; one of our missionary colleagues was to come to Madras for a week-end of special ministry. Would we have cash in hand to feed our colleague for that week-end? At breakfast-time on the day our friend was due to arrive, Marty announced that all our cash was spent. I warned her not to buy anything. The suspense of the testing time was acute but did not last long. Early in the morning our handyman came to the bungalow. He contacted Marty and handed her six Rupees. "What's this?", Marty enquired. He replied, "Amma, several months ago the master gve me two worn-out car batteries to sell when an opportunity offered. Well, a man just turned up and bought both of them for six Rupees". A joint etc., were purchased and I don't think our visitor noticed anything unusual about our diet. The experiment was a great blessing and encouragement and we were profoundly thankful.

The earliest picture of David Thrower, around 1921.

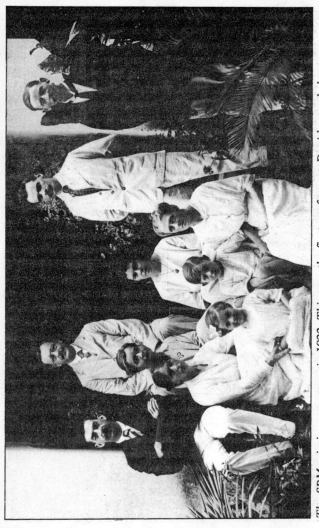

The SBM missionary group in 1922. This was the first conference David attended.

Missionary group in 1927, which was the first conference attended by Mary.

David and Marty on furlow in England, with son Vivian, 1929.

Mission bungalow in Kilpauk, Madras, where the Throwers lived when in Madras.

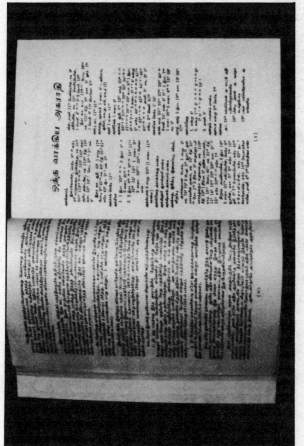

David's Tamil Concordance

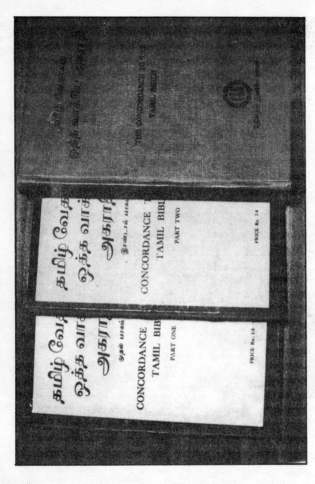

Parts 1 and 2 and the combined Tamil Concordance.

Family group in India, around 1945.

Family group in England, around 1949/50.

Last picture of David and Marty together before Marty's death in 1980.

The first section of David's Tamil Concordance was published in 1943. (The entire work came out in 1960). With over 170,000 entries it is the first such concordance to be publshed in any Indian language.

But the accumulation of the strains of wartime and of what the Apostle Paul called "the care of all the churches" left David with a nervous breakdown. This made an extended furlough necessary so that he and Marty were away from India from early 1952 until November 1953.

Out of this apparent setback the Lord brought good. It came to be realised that not only had David's load been too great a strain for him to bear but that the whole business of a non-Indian overseeing churches – David had been looking after five churches as well as numerous schools – was unbiblical. Although it was carried on with the best intentions such a policy was a departure from the original missionary ideals. The impetus grew to make Indian churches self-governing. More recent events have shown that this important change came not a moment too soon. From now on missionaries were to be helps to the work, not superintendents of it.

David regarded his illness as only an interlude before he could throw himself back into his life's work. He returned not so much a leader of missionaries but as the main source of literature in Tamil, of Christian words that would "bear silent witness to the Gospel in places where no missionary had been".

4.
War and peace

Wartime conditions, such as the partial evacuation of Madras, air-raid precautions and black-outs restricted our out-of-doors activities. However this provided more time for desk work in the bungalow and especially for additional work on Concordance compilation. In fact, with the assistance of several Tamil brethren I was able to collect and arrange the references to hundreds of Biblical names, while Brother Benjamin gave his undivided attention to the more complicated task of dealing with Bible topics.

What a day of rejoicing it was when, in Septemberr 1943, precisely twenty years after I started to compile the Concordance to the Tamil Bible, the first batch of copies of Part 1 were received from the publishers. We had a tea-party for all who had helped us in the work, and I made a little speech, although the printing had to stop at that point as no more printing paper was available, nor could it be imported until peace returned.

For us the paramount event of 1943 was the devastating deluge that inundated the whole of Madras city and a vast area of the surrounding countryside. It was the most wide-spread and destructive flood in living memory, stretching along the coast the full length of the ten-mile-long city and inland a distance of about twenty-five miles. A number of people were drowned and others electrocuted by fallen power cables. An unknown number of cattle were washed away. At least seventy five thousand people were rendered homeless, their huts or houses having collapsed. Some lost the little they had in the mud that took over the sites of their homes. There were dozens of military camps in the outskirts of the city where men were being trained for jungle warfare in Burma. These suffered much damage and some were completely destroyed.

Water covered most of the city for two or three days, and our compound in Kilpauk had four feet of water in the higher ground and eight feet in the lower parts. No newspapers were published for several days as the printing machines were under water; the same applied to the turbines at the electricity station, so there was no supply of electric current for a day or two. I was due to preach at Ayanapuram but no such activity was possible that day and in the early morning the water was lapping the steps of our front verandah. Within two or three hours the swirling floodtide came pouring through the open windows and filled the ground floor rooms to a depth of four feet. Light furniture floated and from time to time banged against the walls. Numerous small articles such as stools with wooden handles disappeared through the windows.

There were seven of us in the house at the time, five ladies and two men. For the rest of that day and the following night we seven had to take refuge in our one upstairs room. It was therefore a case of all hands to the pump, transporting foodstuffs, crockery and books upstairs for our use or before they were ruined by the rising tide. During the morning our friends at the village of Ayanapuram, outside the flooded area, somehow got a message to us to the effect that our old bungalow might collapse; why not come to Ayanapuram and be safe? We tried to do this but soon after leaving the compound we were all swept off the road by the powerful current and across a deep gully and were on our way to the Bay of Bengal, but, providentially, one of our number had the presence of mind to take along a length of rope; this we threw round a large tree and six of us hung on to it, whilst Mrs Brand took refuge on the top of a compound wall!

Several Tamil men saw our plight, came to our rescue and accompanied us back to our compound. We then slowly waded back home, except for one of our lady visitors and Marty who struck out and swam to the house; snakes, mud and debris notwithstanding! After that we all decided to stay put for the duration. During that night I frequently looked at the water level on the garage door and noted that the flood began to recede slowly during the early hours of Monday. I think that, by God's mercy, there was no loss of life among our Tamil Baptist friends, but a number of families had their homes severely damaged. It took us six months to restore complete normality for ourselves, and much longer to do what was possible to assist our many Indian folk who were still worse affected.

One of my duties was to teach the church leaders how to conduct the business side of their church life, which included the disciplining of members when necessary. In this connection, I was faced with the apparently insoluable problem of ejecting a family from a house in one of our villages. The people had unlawfully occupied the place year after year, but all our effort to persuade them to move had failed. There seemed to be no redress, apart from litigation. As I was not prepared to comtemplate this, I was greatly distressed about the matter.

Then one day, I read again in Matthew 18 of our Lord's directions for dealing with such a situation. Having unsuccessfully tried the earlier moves outlined there, I decided to "tell it to the church" at Ayanapuram, to which the offending person belonged. This I proceeded to do, at which someone proposed that the offending man be given one month in which to vacate the premises, failing which he would be excommunicated. It was resolved that this should be done. The month passed, but nothing happened. Then my monthly visit to the church came round again. I noticed the offending member in the chapel, and that as the Communion service was about to start, he moved from his seat. He did not share in that service, nor did he cause any disturbance, as some expected. Soon after my return to the bungalow, I was visited by a friend who explained that given another ten days, he would return the key. I readily agreed, and before the ten days had elapsed, the offending man himself came and handed me the key of the house and asked my pardon. How we thanked the Lord for all His goodness in this matter, for he had worked wonders in response to our obedience to His Word!

Unhappily Marty was unable to cope with our situation in the closing months of 1945. It had been a difficult six years for both of us under wartime conditions. Marty spent eleven days in hospital after which she was nursed and cared for at the Mission house pending our homeward voyage for furlough. Continued treatment, rest and loving care enabled Marty to recover sufficiently to undertake the rail journey to Bombay and face the journey home.

Just prior to leaving Madras we examined the church rolls to see how many Indian friends had received baptism during the six years of our term of service, and to our profound joy and gratitude, we found that the Lord had blessed the Madras Tamil churches with one hundred and seventy five new members. The fact that all these people made a personal confession of faith in the Lord Jesus Christ as their Saviour before the assembed members of their churches is great cause for thanksgiving. Also a number of friends had been accepted by the churches and awaited immersion at the time of our departure.

After several hours standing in a queue waiting to see the various officials we made our way up the gangplank of the "Georgia". Marty was completely exhausted and longed to

reach our cabin and lie down. But nothing so pleasing was
in store for as soon as we reached the ship's deck, an officer
met us and asked us to stay where we were because the
ship's Medical Officer wanted to see me. It wasn't long
before the doctor came and informed me that if we travelled
by that ship Marty would have to occupy a dormitory with
twenty other women, while I would have similar
accommodation in a men's compartment. He added that
such accommodation was quite unsuitable for my wife's
needs; she was travelling on a high priority medical
certificate and must have some comfort. After a heartfelt
sigh, there was nothing for it but for us to retrace our steps
down to the quay and wait for a vessel that could provide
more suitable berths. By this time Marty could hardly
stand; she did, however, manage to walk to a taxi which
took us back to the station which we had left a few hours
earlier. There I put her on a settee in a waiting-room and
made arrangements for a meal.

Then I began to wonder where we were to go from there!
At first I thought we knew no one in Bombay who could
help us. Then I remembered our friends Tom and Beth
Ashworth who formerly worked for a period at a cotton-mill
in Kovilpatti and became friendly with the missionaries in
that area. They were now at one of their company's mills in
Bombay; but which one! That we did not know. Moreover
we soon learned that there were two firms with practically
the same name that had mills in Bombay! Marty rested on
the settee the remainder of that day while I made a number
of visits to the telephone exchange just outside the railway
station in my efforts to contact Tom and Beth. It was a day
of agonising frustration for I did not know which of the two
companies was my friends' one.

"No, we have no-one of the name of Ashworth in any of
mills" I was told. Then I tried one after another of the mills
of the other firm and eventually after almost giving up hope,

I heard Beth's voice at the other end of the line. As soon as she heard of our predicament she said: "Just cross over from the Main Line Station to the Suburban Electric system, get on a train and alight at Parel Station. Tom and I will be there to meet you". What an unspeakable relief: Putting our heavy baggage in the Left Luggage Office, we boarded an electric train for Parel. It was the evening rush-hour and I had difficulty coping with Marty's needs of help and our suitcases. We also had to travel in two separate compartments but, almost miraculously, I managed to get the two of us, plus the bags out of the train at Parel, before it started off again. Our good friends took the two waifs in and kept them a fortnight.

On one of the two Sundays that we were in the mill at Parel, our friend Tom sent me in his car to one of the Tamil churches in Bombay for the morning service. I was the first member of the congregation to arrive. Within a few minutes an elderly man came in and enquired whether I could speak Tamil and, if so, would I take the sermon. He explained that the minister was away and he had to lead the service. He would therefore be glad if I could help him out, which I was very happy to do. After a delightful two weeks in the home of Tom and Beth, we went aboard the S.S. "City of Exeter" on our 28th Wedding Anniversary, just before Christmas. Marty had no difficulty coping with the formalities this time and we had an uneventful voyage. How good is the God we adore! – although He sometimes moves in a mysterious way, His wonders to perform!

That year's Annual Report featured a brief contribution by me that concluded – "After our arrival in the Homeland we greatly appreciated three months rest, most of it amid rural scenes. The wonderful revival of apparently dead trees and plants enacted before our eyes during the spring was a parable of the equally miraculous raising to life of dead souls which we long to see performed everywhere in

Tamilnadu". During this furlough we illustrated many of
our messages by using a thousand feet of cine film depicting
the work in Tamilnadu. This furlough held another unique
experience for Marty and me for we were separated for most
of our time in Britian! Our home was in London, but Marty
was not physically fit to do the housekeeping, and she
needed a period for convalescence in a rural setting. Two
unmarried cousins of mine who lived in Herefordshire came
to her aid. By their kindness Marty went to stay with them
and learnt something about their fruit cultivation. The visit
eventually lasted over a year. Marty steadily improved in
health until, when the winter came and the village was cut
off by snow-drifts, she stood in for the local pastor of a small
church, conducting the Sunday services, playing the
harmonium and attending to all the tasks connected with
the ministry until the pastor was able to return.

All this was ideal for Marty, but what about my need of a
home and base from which I could continue my deputation
work! I was accommodated by friends at Leytonstone, who
treated me as one of the family. My location at Leytonstone
a hundred yards from Wanstead Flats, was to prove an
ideal one before 1946 was out. The Mission Council decided
that the General Secretary, should pay a visit to Tamilnadu
for five months from November. Council also resolved that I
be given an extension of furlough and serve as Acting
Secretary during his absence. The Secretary's home and
office were just a few yards from Wanstead Flats on their
eastern side, while I was twenty minutes walk across the
Flats to the Mission Office to attend to the mail.

One special joy for Marty and me during the furlough
was the baptism of our son, Vivian. He had loved the Lord
since he was a small boy, but the ministry of the Word in
the summer of that year was so powerfully blessed to him
that he felt challenged to confess his faith publicly by
baptism. The pastor of the local church invited me to

preach at his chapel on that occasion and to conduct Vivian's immersion. However, I did not feel able to do the latter, but I preached on the text! "He that believeth and is baptised shall be saved", pointing out that, while the Saviour, in the same sentence as my text stated that faith is the one essential thing, public confession of that faith by baptism saves us from the sin of disobedience and also helps to keep us from many another snare in our Christian life.

The following two months were momentous ones for India. Lord Mountbatten was putting the finishing touches to his plan to enable the British to disengage themselves from ruling this vast land. Political partition gave the Hindus and Muslims separate states and India celebrated her Independence Day on 15th August 1947. That day, the Namakkal Tamil Baptist church bell was rung before 5 am and a rocket was fired on the Rock. We held a service of Thanksgiving in the church at 6 o'clock in the morning, and the members of the church and congregation had a feast at noon. There was also the function of hoisting India's new tricolour flag, sports for the boys of the Hostel, and sweets for the school children.

I was only in the Salem area for four or five months and, in Novemeber went up to Madras to meet Marty. When I met her at the railway station I thought she looked extremely fit and was very thankful for the good recovery she had made. Then a little later on I suffered an alarming collapse while preparing for bed. Marty called the doctor and although it was late in the evening he very kindly came at once and, after examining me, said he thought it may be a coronary thrombosis, so he promised to bring a heart specialist from the hospital the next day. This he did and the specialist found my pulse much more regular than it had been the previous night. His verdict was that it was definitely not thrombosis, but he ordered one week's rest in bed followed by a slow return to normal activity. I was not to do a full day's work for a month, but by God's goodness my health steadily improved until I was quite fit again.

Three weeks later, Marty and I were able to go to the beach for an hour or two, I was still taking it easy. On the bus that brought us home we noticed that our fellow passengers were conversing in subdued tones about something very serious. We asked one of them what it was and learned that Mahatma Gandhi, the Father of the Nation, had been shot and killed in Delhi while we were sitting on the beach. This tragedy shook India more than anything that happened during the long struggle for independence. He who had been the uncrowned ruler of Indian heart's had gone.

I was able to attend the Annual Conference that year, provided I took precautions to conserve my strength. Owing to my weakness I gave only one message, that being, "We have this treasure in earthen vessels". At that moment my earthen vessel was extremely weak and fragile, but the treasure it contained was as great as ever! Then we received a token of the Lord's treasure in connection with our journey. Physically I certainly needed as comfortable a trip as possible and when we reached the railway station we found a most extraordinary scene. The place was almost deserted and we had a compartment on the train to ourselves almost all the way with maximum comfort. And the reason? It was the day of the immersion of Gandhi's ashes in the great rivers of India and in the sea, so the City's population had flocked to the beach for this function and travel was forgotten!

April and May are normally the hottest months of the year in Madras; maximum temperatures are above the century mark most days. 1948 was a particularly hot year, the mercury rising about 107g F on a number of occasions. Minimum readings also are high at such times. It is not so much the temperature itself that makes the Madras climate rather trying, the humidity is a still more potent factor in this matter and on one occasion I noted that it read 97g F.

That year we planned to have our hot weather holiday at Coonoor on the Nilgiris. The journey from Madras was made by the Blue Mountains Express train. After a good overnight run, the train reached Mettupalayam near the foot of the Nilgiri Hills on schedule in the early morning. There we boarded the train of the hill railway for the long climb that is so steep that a rack and pinion system has to be used to prevent trains from slipping. All went well for a few miles, after which the train suddenly stopped far from any station. We were in a deep and narrow ravine flanked by rocks. The rack and pinion device had jammed so that the train could neither move forward nor backward. Although it was only early morning, the heat was unbearable and neither food nor drink were available there in the middle of the mountainside jungle. The drinking water that we had with us was soon consumed. Eventually we hit upon a life saver, for we managed to have some boiled water from the Engine which enabled us to keep going!

This was the fourth breakdown in which I had been involved, on four different Indian railways, and this time I was not in very good fettle for the ordeal. Eventually help was obtained, the damaged part removed and the train made its way back to Mettupalayam during the evening. There we were put aboard buses and got up to Coonoor late in the evening. No taxis were available then but a friendly lorry driver kindly took us on board to our destination, arriving there around 11 pm, instead of at noon! What a day it had been!

Later in that year of breakdowns Marty became involved in a special piece of service resulting from yet another threatened collapse. Early in June a serious situation arose on the Kolli Hills; well-nigh riot conditions set in. The local hill workers of the Mission expressed their determination to be rid of the members of the staff who came from the Plains. The latter of course reacted violently to this. The future of our service to the people of the Kolli Hills was in jeopardy. My health did not permit me to become actively involved in the matter, but Marty with others were able to visit the Kollis. They were to endeavour to bring about a just and peaceful settlement of the trouble. It was obvious that the situation was such that the local missionary could not be expected to handle it without assistance. God in His great goodness gave the members of the deputation the needful tact, patience and insight to deal with this potentially dangerous situation successfully. They decided that all workers from the Plains be withdrawn from the Kolli Hills and redeployed in other areas of our ministry in Tamilnadu. All parties involved agreed to this decision which was implemented and the trouble settled amicably.

Before the end of the year we were faced with breakdown number four. Two missionary couples serving in Tamilnadu were in a state of broken fellowship, and collagues demanded that the Conference chairman do something about it. However, the chairman had no intention of making things worse by using the hammer and wrench method. I desired to wait till I felt the time was ripe for meaningful action. When this point had been reached I asked both couples to meet me at Trichinapalli Junction. It was a good centre for us all to reach and it also had good facilities such as a restaurant and retiring rooms where we could stay and meet without being disturbed. Marty and I were prepared to have separate talks with each of the couples, but in the event I just led a brief devotional session for the six of us, using Joshua of old as an example of how God can bring victory out of defeat. Then the senior of the men gave me the key of his room and asked Marty and me to wait there while he and his wife joined the others in their room. We got to our knees and remained in earnest prayer for our four colleagues until they called us, over an hour later, to say that the trouble between them had been settled. The subject of their conversation was never revealed to us, nor did we say anything concerning it to any of them. All I did was to bring the parties together; the Lord did the rest.

Happily the year closed on a more positive note, for during December, the Madras churches held their first Conference, when delegates from the various groups spent three days in fellowship. It was obvious that such annual united assemblies provided a much-needed boost to the morale of the believers and Christian workers, the vast majority of whom spend their lives and labour in a certain amount of isolation. About that period Marty had an interesting experience. One day the Lord clearly instructed her to "sell all". She said she could sell everything except the rat trap: that was an essential piece of equipment in constant use. She also asked the Lord to send us purchasers. It wasn't long before an American friend of ours called. She saw Marty and told her, "I was one of those who sold everything they had and left India after the country was given independence. All missionaries were expected to leave shortly anyway. After a while, however, I learned that foreign workers were still carrying on here. So I have come back. I have a nice little car but nothing else. I have rented a flat in Vepery; have you any furniture to spare that will help to furnish it?" Marty took our friend from room to room, repeating like a refrain, "Is there anything in here that you would like?" We were relieved of several things that we did not use a great deal and did not really need. She took a dining table and a few other articles. Shortly after that the Lord gave Marty the assurance that He had accepted her act of obedience. She need not sell anything more. Marty was later able to note, "The general tone of life today in the city and the surge of changing events have been buffeting us and our hope for the future. Thousands of Europeans have left India, nevertheless a more certain hope is being born out of the turmoil and uncertainty of these days. Twenty one sisters have passed through the waters of baptism during the past year. For these tokens of the Lord's blessing we praise Him. In a city such as Madras, where nearly all the isms of Christendom appear to congregate, our people need all the armour of the Christian warfare."

This was written less than three years after India gained independence and only a matter of months before the country was to become a Republic. Hence the uncertainty pervading the Indian scene at that time.

Thursday 26th January 1950 was to be one of the most outstanding dates in India's history. It was the day on which this great country became a sovereign democratic republic. The new constitution that came into force then contains a clause of special interest to Christians, one which conferred on all citizens the right to profess, practice and propogate their religion, which proved a great encouragement to us.

This new year also opened with special services for the dedication of Tamil brothers to ministry in a number of churches. These were steps of great progress and we rejoiced with our friends in these signs of indigenous church life. We looked forward with hope to similar progress in other areas.

We in Madras did not have to wait long for these hopes to be realized, at least in part, for in April we had the satisfaction of appointing Samual Devanesam (the father of the present Samuel Devanesam, pastor in Kilpauk) as pastor of the church at Vepery. When giving his testimony, Samuel stated that he was led to see the need of personal faith in the Lord Jesus Christ by reading a sermon by C H Spurgeon and that later he saw the need of believer's baptism through another sermon of that prince of

preachers, leading him to be baptised in a river near
Madras.

Eight years after the publication of the first section of the
"Concordance to the Tamil Bible", the second became
available in May 1951. A task which I had vowed to God to
complete, had taken nearly thirty years of two men's labour.
And here it was! Unbelievable! Finished at last! This
necessary study book, is a topical, not verbal, concordance
and therefore serves as an essential work of reference for all
versions of the Tamil Bible. The book later became a single
volume containing about one hundred and seventy
thousand references to some eight thousand four hundred
biblical topics and names.

Our diligence has been well rewarded, for revised
editions were required on no less than four occasions in
1954, '62, '76 and '82. I then proceeded to place copies of
the Concordance in the Bodleian Library, Oxford, the
library of Cambridge University, the British Museum
Library of Oriental Manuscripts and the library of London
University School of Oriental Studies.

One Sunday later in the year, I preached at the Tamil
church in Royapuram, Madras. While I was delivering the
message I developed a pain in my chest, but was able to
complete my sermon. On returning home I had to go to bed
and call a doctor. He found that I was suffering from a
functional disease of the heart but did not know what
caused it. He enquired how soon we would leave for Britain
and we told him that we were booked to sail from Bombay
the following March. When he heard that he assured us that
he could get me on my feet in good time for us to travel as
planned.

In order to give me additional relief from the noise and
bustle of the main bungalow Marty arranged for me to
occupy a small room in a corner of the compound. As I was

being carried there Pastor Devanesam, who lived in the compound, came to me and said, "Remember, Ayya (Sir) – it is 'in quietness and confidence lies your strength". That spiritual meditation probably did me more good than the doctor's treatment, although one thing the physician recommended was that I should drink plenty of milk, and so our own milch goats became most important.

When we left India in March 1952 we took with us a letter from our Madras doctor to a friend of his who was a heart specialist at University College Hospital, London.

The fifteen years covered in this chapter mark the last phase of David's work in India before his 'retirement'. After their return from furlough the Throwers lived in a series of rural retreats in the Nilgiri hills, a sharp contrast with the busyness of the city of Madras.

Literature work was increasingly important. The concordance was finished, though not yet published in full. Much else needed doing. David wrote and published a devotional commentary on the Minor Prophets and some tracts were printed on his small press. Marty helped to distribute the literature. David's advise on Tamil matters was increasingly sought by other missionaries.

In the middle of this period of quiet work there came another upheaval. The process of making the Indian churches self-governing made it necessary to transfer the Mission's various properties into Indian hands. But how? In what way? The Indians clamoured for ownership. Eventually it was decided to form four separate trusts, one in each area of Mission work, in an effort to safeguard some measure of independency for the churches. For over a year during 1967-8 David, who had been granted the power of attorney, was in the thick of the tangled legal procedures.

These changes marked the end of an era. The days of British Christian paternalism in India were fast disappearing. The attempt to reproduce the details of English Strict Baptist culture in India were abandoned. From now on there were to be 'Indian forms of the fruit of the Spirit'. And, as several missionaries withdrew from India for a variety of reasons, the Mission itself ceased to be exclusively Tamil-centred.

5.
The end of an era

In the opening days of March 1952, Ruth Harris, Marty and I sailed from Bombay. It was a comfortable and speedy voyage, and we landed in Britain fifteen days after leaving India. Shortly after our arrival I spent two weeks in the University College Hospital where I was thoroughly examined by the heart specialist. The specialist carried out numerous tests and sent a voluminous report to the Mission Secretary. The cardiologist could find nothing wrong with me and every test produced a negative result. I did not take any drugs whatever at the hosptial, but after about ten days of rest in bed, and good food, my heart began to function normally once more. Unfortunately for the specialist this rather dramatic change in my condition occurred a few hours before his students were to be given a bedside lecture on a normal heart functioning in an abnormal manner due to an unknown cause. The good man was greatly upset by the development and appeared to decide that my case was nothing more than one of malingering. He wanted to recommend that the Mission send me back to my work at once. But the House Physician who was more directly responsible for my care said: "Mr Thrower, we know that you have been under heavy strain in the tropics for many years. We are going to recommend that you be given six months total rest." Then he added a word of personal advice: "Go into the country and collect wild flowers", and I did just that; one of the results being a modest herbarium of British wild flowers.

We spent most of that furlough with our old home of Clapham as our base. During the latter part of the time Marty underwent minor surgery followed by some time in a hospital in Surrey for convalescence. Altogether she was away five weeks. In the meantime my engagements were fulfilled, I visited Marty each week at Cobham and catered for Irwin, Olive and myself. Marty's sister, Vera Rippon and family occupied the lower rooms at the old Watts' home while my family lived upstairs. This resulted in our having a somewhat amusing legend attached to the door bells; it read – "Thrower up; Rippon down".

Furlough number five was the longest of our eight regular visits to the UK for deputation ministry and rest, and we were in Britain about twelve months. Although I needed, and was given, a lengthy period of rest and recuperation after the breakdown, I was enabled to fulfil many Mission engagements during the last part of the furlough.

During our return trip, we became friendly with five lady missionaries, bound for different parts of India. An amusing incident occurred as we seven went ashore as a group at Port Said: down the gangway and across the pontoon bridge. When we returned I stood at the bottom of the gangway while the six ladies filed up. One of the ship's officers came by and remarked: "Oh, are they your chickens?" I replied: "No, they are my ducklings!" After that I was known as Father Drake, Marty became Mother Duck and the other five were our ducklings! A few days later the ladies purchased a mechanical duck at Aden, which they presented to Marty and me just before we reached Bombay.

We reached Bombay at the beginning of December and covered the eight hundred miles to Madras by train in about thirty hours. The following Thursday we left by a night train for Sattur in the Ramnad District and thence to Paniadipatti, by bus for most of the way, then by bullock-cart. The name Paniadipatti means the village under the palmyras. Nine of our places of worship can be seen from the terraced roof of the Paniadipatti bungalow, and it was my privilege to preach the Word in one or other of these villages almost every Sunday for the next three years. We often walked to the villages on Sundays, but for the more distant places used springed bullock-cart and hired bulls for traction from a local farmer.

During each week my time was fully occupied with the development of Tamil literature production, and of course we also did some outreach in the form of colportage as we moved about the area at weekends. Also during that year my literature work included the translation and printing of a number of leaflet tracts. Ours was now a quiet rural life, for the bungalow was not even situated in the village but stood in its own compound a quarter of a mile away. Our routine was therefore in striking contrast to the busy life that we led in the Madras area in earlier days. There we had meetings almost every evening of the week; here, nothing of that kind.

We did enjoy a pleasant diversion, however, when Marty and I went to attend an evangelistic campaign conducted by Dr Billy Graham, who spoke to a crowd of at least forty thousand in a well organised open-air meeting place. People assembled from every direction, some travelling great distances to attend the meetings. The number that came out to be counselled varied but averaged three thousand at each meeting. The great gatherings, and Dr Graham's simple, straightforward presentation of the Gospel message were greatly inspiring, but it appeared that quite a proportion of those counselled did not really know what it was all about; it was obvious that many went forward simply to have a close-up view of the great preacher.

I was able to make fair progress with my Tamil literature work during the middle half of the year, but the concluding portion of 1956 saw another stirring up of our nest. In June

our youngest son, Irwin, suffered a nervous breakdown.
Marty felt she should go to England and help him in his
time of need. We therefore placed the matter before the
Council. Permission was granted for her to take leave for
this purpose. We had recently taken a small cottage at
Kotagiri, on the Nilgiri Hills, on a five year lease as a
holiday residence. We therefore visited Kotagiri and
prepared the house, known as 'Lyle Cottage' for my
occupation for the duration of my grass-widowerhood. We
then returned to Paniadipatti to do our packing. Finally, we
set out, Marty heading for London, and me for 'Lyle
Cottage', and our separate lives.

I did not have to endure complete isolation for long as
the Lord had a delightful surprise in store for me. Six days
after my arrival I was joined in the cottage by brother D
Dorairaj who had been the preacher at our Sembiam
church but had now been invited by the Kotagiri Tamil
Baptist church to serve them as Pastor. Dorairaj had left his
family in Madras, where his wife Hephzibah was
headmistress of a Christian School. It was, therefore, an
ideal arrangement for him to live with me at 'Lyle' with the
chapel next door. The Lord thus graciously provided me
with a companion for my first three months in Kotagiri. I
had known Brother Dorairaj well since the year 1940, and
Hephzibah almost as long. I officiated at their marriage in
1943 and have been in close touch with their family ever
since.

At Paniadipatti I often used a moped as my means of
transport. It was extremely useful for getting around the
area, although I had a few tumbles on sandy patches of the
narrow paths. Marty also had a moped but was not able to
use it under these conditions, but she frequently
accompanied me when visiting the villages 'by walk' as the
Tamils say; also when I used the bullock-cart. At Kotagiri
the question of transport called for a different solution. On

an undulating plateau of nearly seven thousand feet, with a few level patches of road the use of a cycle or moped is subject to serious limitation. Here either a scooter, motor-cycle or car are the best types of vehicle. However, here in the late fifties we did not greatly need transport as my work was of a sedentary nature.

A year or two earlier I had prepared pamphlets containing studies in the Minor Prophets for use in monthly Bible study classes. These were now reprinted in book form. As the outcome of writing competitions conducted through the church magazine 'Deepikai ('light'), we had also produced several small booklets for children. A number of other items had been produced and were in circulation. I carried on writing, translating, and proof-reading, during these difficult days without the support and encouragement of Marty.

Then my sight, which for many years had been unaccountably growing weaker, began to fail more seriously. In earlier years Marty helped by reading for me, but she was not available this time. So I was presented with another crisis, for I had tried so many doctors and hospitals without discovering what was wrong. Well, I decided to go to the Christian hospital in Kotagiri and saw an eye surgeon of long experience. Numerous tests were carried out with the result that it was found that I had both chronic and acute amoebic dysentery. A preliminary course of medication was prescribed, after which I went into hospital. During this time the doctors worked wonders and I came out a new man. However, the trouble shortly afterwards threatened to return. It was recommended that I have a second course of injection of emetine, the specific drug for amoebic dysentery. I would, I was assured, then have no further trouble from the amoeba, which was described as 'Public Enemy No.1,' The injections were given and, from that day to this, I have enjoyed such health as I had not

known for decades. How I thank the Lord for those good
doctors.'

My time as a grass-widower drew to a close soon after
the beginning of 1958, on my return to Britain. It was a
comfortable voyage with an interesting trip ashore at
Naples, where I visited the semi-extinct volcano, Salfatara,
and saw boiling sand and steam issuing from the ground.
We finally docked at Southampton early in March and
proceeded to Waterloo where a goodly number of relatives
and friends met us. Marty was, of course, among them, and
our third long separation was over.

As usual, it wasn't long before I was engaged in visits to
the churches in various parts of the country, and in my
spare time I did a certain amount of translation of books
and booklets into Tamil, concentrating on items that are
much needed, but for which it is difficult to find time while
on foreign soil. That reminded me that I had been involved
in translation work to some extent ever since the mid-
twenties , and at this time I was able to write: "If, during
our early days in India, we had been told we should soon be
producing Tamil literature for a ready market we would
certainly have found it hard to believe. But a glance at the
book-list illustrates the wide range of readers for whom
literature is now being prepared by our Mission. The
catalogue is divided into a dozen sections. The time has
come for us rapidly to expand our output in this field. We
started to tackle the problem seriously three and a half years
ago. As a result, the number of our publications has already
been doubled, and the range of the material considerably
broadened. One item that appeals to Christian workers
beyond our borders is the commentary on the last twelve
books of the Old Testament. It sold out within nine months
of its appearance. The reason for this lay in the fact that an
Indian Bishop was so convinced of the value of the book
that he instructed his presbyters throughout the area to

commence weekly Bible classes for their congregations, to
study the Minor Prophets with the aid of these lessons. A
large order was received from the Danish Missionary
Society, but by that time our stock was exhausted. A second
impression was therefore printed. Before leaving India in
February we witnessed considerable progress in this field,
steady expansion characterising both the production and
distribution of our publications".

Marty and I had a busy round of deputation tours till the
late spring of 1959, Council having generously given us an
extension of furlough for family reasons. After some time,
Irwin was taken under the care of some good friends of ours,
so that we were able to resume our work in South India
during the summer of 1959.

We left Britain for the seventh time in late June. After we
spent a night with Vivian and Betty in their home, they took
us and our baggage to Southampton. Sailing by the s.s.
'Corfu', we disembarked at Colombo in mid-July. This visit
took place during the south-west monsoon; at a time when
the Island normally had one hundred and eighty inches of
rain, so there was a torrential downpour throughout our
stay. But this did not deter us from visiting the gem-mine
workings and seeing the rubies on sale in the shops. Nor did
the rain prevent us from visiting cooly 'lines' on three tea
estates for evangelistic outreach. Both Marty and I spoke at
these meetings, nearly all the labourers being Tamils.

From Colombo we proceeded to Kotagiri to resume our
Tamil literature work. We had been sent to Kotagiri
because none of the Mission bungalows on the Plains was
available for our occupation. The tiny holiday cottage,
'Lyle', had served well enough while I was alone during the
last year and a half in Tamilnadu, but now that there were
two of us it was not quite so easy and it took us some time to
become accustomed to the rather cramped quarters of
'Lyle' Cottage after living and working in the spacious

rooms of Mission houses for thirty five years. So before long we purchased a large garden umbrella which constituted my office and study at all times except the monsoon period. I quickly picked up the threads of the work that had been interrupted by the furlough; there was much translating, revising and fair-copying of manuscripts, corresponding with printers, and proof reading to be done, so that a great many books and booklets were newly issued or reprinted.

Marty was faced with a more complicated problem than I. All I had to do was carry on and develop the same type of work as before under changed conditions. But in Marty's case it wasn't so simple. She felt the need for a new avenue of service suited to this mountain area where none of the women's meetings, girls' Bible classes or personal ministry to women and girls living in the compound were open to her. However, it wasn't long before she decided that she should complement my work of literature production by developing the distribution of books and booklets in the tea estates and tribal villages of the Kotagiri area. A potential colporteur was also ready at hand, for our house-help was always happy when asked to 'go places'. Thangam was given a day's leave from housework each week to go out selling books. After the first such effort she returned completely frustrated, for she had only sold one booklet and handed Marty a quarter of an anna, that is one sixtyfourth of a rupee'. However, our book seller persevered and, during the next few years, disposed of thousands of items.

Marty also wished to demonstrate to would-be part-time colporteurs that it was possible to engage in this type of Christian service without looking to someone else to finance their effort. From the start, therefore, her Literature Auxiliaries account – as she called it – was solely financed by the discount allowed by publishers and bookshops on books purchased. This account is still functioning and, from time to time provides funds for printing projects.

Thangam covered a considerable area in her weekly outings for colportage. She also occasionally had opportunities for book-selling at special meetings in Kotagiri. For instance, when a popular poet-singer conducted a series of Gospel meetings in her little town Tangam was given permission to display her books in the hall. The visiting speaker bought a book each evening, read it before the next meeting and then publicly advertised our literature, particularly urging the people to buy and read the book that he had read with profit. Many sales resulted from that kind assistance.

A very different experience was when Thangam visited a tribal village and was attacked by a mad dog. She stood her ground and prayed hard. Then she held out her umbrella to protect herself; the animal bit the end off it! Our good helper escaped without being bitten although she was somewhat crestfallen on her return with only half an umbrella! She several times visited a tea estate where, a few years later, a son of the manager was killed by a wild elephant.

It was now eight years since the Mission set me apart for full-time work in this field of books, booklets, tracts, book markers and text cards, and during this time we had produced a number of items not issued in Tamil by other Christian publishers. These included simple Bible stories and other material suitable for children. Both production and sales continuously expanded although, regrettably, the former faster than the latter, for the reading habit is slow in developing among newly-literate Tamils.

At our field Conference in February 1960 our guest speaker was Ernest Kevan, Principal of The London Bible College. Dr Kevan gave us four valuable studies in the subject of the Lord's supper, which we later published in English and Tamil. Before leaving the Nilgiris he visited us for an hour or two in our cottage at Kotagiri. That was a very happy occasion, as Ernest and I had played with our Meccano sets together when we were boys.

Immediately after the Conference all our colleagues came to Kotagiri for the wedding of two of our number. Marty and I had been asked to stand in for the bride's parents, which we were delighted to do. We decorated the hall with dozens of lovely arum lilies, which could be found in plentiful supply, growing wild around the town. Marty was particularly pleased that she managed to secure a joint of ham from a local farm, for the reception.

In the middle of 1963 the Thrower family nest was stirred once more; but this time it was a more pleasant experience than some earlier ones. Although the accommodation at 'Lyle Cottage' was really inadequate for our needs nothing more suitable appeared to be available in Kotagiri, so we had learned to cope fairly well with life and work there. Then, about June, a retired lady who occupied a roomy flat in a large house up the hill above 'Lyle' moved away and was kind enough to recommend the owners to let the flat to us. We moved to the flat (in the house 'Mistley') and found it a big step up on 'Lyle' in more ways than one. Not only did it provide better accommodation but also its location was very helpful. At 'Lyle' we had a long, stiff climb every time we wanted to go anywhere, whereas at 'Mistley' we were much nearer the public road. We continued literature production and distribution from the 'Mistley' flat for about eight months and then left for our seventh furlough, which was an exceptionally full one for both Marty and me. Quite apart from official Mission engagements we covered a surprising amount of mileage by car, coach and train, renewing and deepening friendships made during the previous six visits in the Old Country.

Immediately on our return, after nine months, we had to engage in some more house-hunting, for 'Mistley' had been

re-let to other people, and there was no room for us. We
therefore considered it more convenient for the future, to try
to buy a house. So we toured the town in search of the house
of God's choice for us. It soon became clear that there were
only three possibilities. Further enquiries eliminated two of
them, leaving 'Danvi' bungalow, one and a half miles north
west of Kotagiri town, as the only available house that was
at all suitable. Within a week of our arrival on the hills we
visitied this house. Both of us saw that, although the
bungalow was in a very run-down condition, it had the
making of a comfortable home and centre for work such as
ours.

But there was one big snag in the venture we were
undertaking. What a fool the prophet Jeremiah was to buy
immovable property when he knew that his country was
about to be invaded by an enemy! What a fool David
Thrower would be to purchase a house and compound in
India when everyone knew that the days of the foreigner in
that land were numbered! Indeed, the prospect was so bad
that many had already left. I am sure many folk, including
some of my own colleagues, called me an errant fool for
doing such a crazy thing. Humanly speaking they were
quite right, and I don't suppose Jeremiah blamed those who
questioned his sanity when he bought his cousin's land on
the eve of an unprecedented national disaster. No, there is
nothing new about God leading His servants from time to
time to act in a way that is inconsistent with common sense.
Reason is sometimes an unreliable guide for the Christian.
Jeremiah's action in obeying God's command in spite of its
apparent folly was in the end fully vindicated. Similarly,
foolish as it was according to human reasoning, my action
in buying the 'Danvi' property has been fully vindicated,
and the property is now worth several times what we paid
for it. Foreigners are not now allowed to own immovable
property in India without Government permission. But the

Government has granted me a license to hold this property as my personal domicile in perpetuity.

The house was more than forty years old but had never had its own water supply. When our Kotagiri friends learned that we were interested in the place they tried to dissuade us from having anything to do with it. "There is no water in the compound" they said. They added the further information that many had attempted to make their residence there but had to give up the bungalow because of the lack of water. So we asked the Lord whether He would give us water there; His reply was given to us, through Isaiah 33:16, where it is stated of God's people that they will live on the heights and among mountain rocks; their bread will be given them and water will not fail them. We bought this house and compound on that last divine promise.

Interestingly enough, 'Danvi' is one of the highest bungalows in Kotagiri and the land is so rocky that the locals know it as 'Stone House'. Marty and I had seen what wonders God can do in the matter of our food supply many years earlier and were sure He would not fail to give us water here. In the event we blasted the rock and struck water at a depth of twelve feet; the nearest wells in the neighbourhood being sixty-five feet and eighty-five feet deep. In later years we deepened the well more than once, but even today it is only about twenty feet deep and often has plenty of water while all the other wells in the area are dry.

How did we choose the site for the well? We contacted a Missionary who was a dowser, a water diviner. After examining the surroundings of the house with his dowsing stick he assured us that there was an abundance of water in a number of places on the plot. Therefore he advised us to locate our well above rather than below the house. We did so and have drawn many thousands of buckets of crystal-clear rock water from the well. Later a cistern was constructed near the well from which the water flows by pipe to all parts of the house. This is a convenience that few houses in Kotagiri possess even today.

Marty got to grips with the many tasks that faced her in our new home, while I picked up the threads of my writing, translating and printing once more, and it was not long before calls for ministry in Tamil churches in various parts of the Nilgiri's began to reach me.

One avenue of usefulness for our Tamil literature that we exploited was the libraries of theological colleges and Bible schools in Tamilnadu. Copies of books were also sent to the libraries of such institutions in other parts of India for the use of Tamils in their student bodies. We also began to receive requests for greetings cards of various kinds which led us to explore the possibility of producing them and a colleague advised us to purchase a small printing machine for this purpose. We were able to purchase a small machine and after some instruction from a local printer, we were able use it on a large variety of jobs.

Soon after we settled at 'Danvi', Marty began to receive appeals for help in cases of sickness, fractures and paralysis from elderly Europeans and Indians living in the town. Sometimes the call came from the person in need and at others from the Superintendent of the local Christian hospital. Once a week, or oftener when necessary, she administered massage or some other form of simple treatment along with a cheery chat. Many persons were helped in this way over a period of several years and Marty found the ministry a pleasant and satisfying one.

In June 1965 I informed the Mission Council of my desire to retire from full-time work at the end of that year. But I offered to render part-time service thereafter if Council so desired. I also applied to the British Government for the usual Retirement Pension and requested that payments be made to the Mission in Britian. So, we were now semi-retired, after many years' hard work. And we needed some rest! That first year back had been a particularly difficult time for us both but the Lord sustained us and we were joyful in our gratitude to Him.

In the mid-sixties there were Christian bookshops in Ootacamund and Coonoor but not in Kotagiri. We therefore explored the possibility of opening a bookroom in our town. This proved to be a long and frustrating experience. Much prayer was offered by ourselves and others regarding two different ways of reaching our objective. We could either purchase a small plot of ground and build, or rent a shop; in the bazaar street. However, nothing came of all our efforts for more than a year. Interested friends made numerous suggestions, bu they all proved non-starters. Then someone noticed a diminutive shop with its shutters up. At first enquiries produced nothing encouraging, for the place was let to a Badega small-holder who sold vegetables and fruits but was unable to pay the rent. However, we met the tenant and explained our need of such a shop as his. The result was that we paid the rent due and took over the little stall. The small-holder responded by supplying us up here at 'Danvi' with vegetables and fruit, and this he did for a number of years.

So the first Christian bookshop in Kotagiri was opened in March 1966 with a simple service of dedication on the roadside. The 'shop' was really only a cubicle with a similar structure on either side. One was a laundry and the other a tailor's workshop. We formed a Bookshop Committee which met monthly to pray for more adequate accommodation. Several friends assisted by serving as part-time salemen, Marty and I also taking our turns at this new post of duty. The bookstall functioned in this way for a little over four years, after which incomparably better accommodation became available.

One day in 1966 we visited Dr Paul Burckhardt, an elderly Swiss missionary who had settled in Kotagiri after a long career as Principal of a theological college in Mangalore on the west coast. During our conversation this friend greatly surprised us by suggesting that we enjoy a rest at his seaside cottage during our cool weather vacations. So we had a delighful holiday at the end of that year within a hundred yards of the Indian Ocean breakers. An epoch-making change took place in the SBM in India in 1967. It was the legal transfer of all Mission properties to the Tamil churches in the four Districts where the latter were located. Both this task and the legal work that followed constituted mammoth undertakings.

After the formation of four Property Trusts the somewhat daunting task of conveying scores of pieces to them fell on the Mission attorney, David Thrower. I contacted a firm of lawyers in Madras and arranged for them to prepare the four Deeds of Transfer for the four Trusts. For this purpose I then gave them all the title deeds of Mission properties, some of which were almost a century old and well-nigh indecipherable. The lawyers took several months to prepare the documents, the details of which I had to check with the utmost care. In a few cases figures used in the old deeds were written in practically obsolete Tamil numerals and symbols and I had to supply a 'key' to those to enable the clerks at the lawyers' office to read them.

Before the end of the year the Deeds were ready to be submitted for registration and a representative of the lawyers accompanied me to the office of the Madras District Registrar. The formalities were completed and, as far as we were concerned, the documents were registered. But alas we soon learned that the Registrar could not finalise the registration until he was supplied with Income Tax Clearance Certificates – one for each Transfer Deed. As the Mission had no income in India there was no question of our being liable for payment of tax, but the formality of the Clearance Certificates had to be attended to. This proved to be a wearisome business that dragged on for nearly a year. Finally, almost in desperation, we appealed to the Commissioner of Income Tax, Madras, the highest authority in Tamilnadu, who cut the Gordian knot for us and the Certificates were handed to me in Ootacamund in the closing days of September 1968. A few days later the Deeds were registered in Madras.

September of that year brought me the unusual experience of preaching to a group of Tamil-speaking folk of the Irula tribe. The chapel in which the service was held was situated in one of my Irula villages in the forest on the edge of the Nilgiris. The Irulas have their own language but it possesses no script. So, in common with those of many other tribal languages, these people have to become literate through Tamil.

Our enjoyable little task that we undertook in the late sixties was that of unofficial chaplains to a Childrens Home in Kotagiri town. Once a week we went to the Home for an hour or two with the Swedish lady Missionary in charge, sharing and praying over the health or problems as they arose among the children and staff. This was both an education and a useful ministry for Marty and me. We also occasionally conducted a service of worship at the Home as all the churches were too far away for some of the children to attend. Also, throughout my career I have, from time to time, been involved in teaching simple accountancy to missionaries and others. Some otherwise well trained workers have found themselves in difficulty when called upon to keep accounts of financial transactions and have come to me for a little tuition in this important subject. Furthermore, many have been the weary hours I have spent tracing an error, or errors in accounts kept by others.

1968 arrived, and with it, the arrival of Norma Steward from Penisula Malaysia, who had requested our help in the understanding of some Tamil language problems. She had the responsibility of supervising the language studies of The Overseas Missionary Fellowship workers preparing for service among Tamils in Malaysia. But she felt unable to fulfil this role efficiently as no-one she contacted in Malaysia could explain adequately the rules governing the conversational form of Tamil needed in work among women and girls in their homes.

Previously, I had received a long list of Tamil queries from her, and the new type of commitment this presented for me was a great pleasure because I had for many years made a study of the constructions peculiar to the colloquial form of our vernacular. My answers produced a second batch of questions, and a third. Now, here she was, having been granted three months' language study leave. During January, Norma and I checked her draft copies of three one-year courses of lessons covering both the literary and colloquial forms, and later Norma sampled the differing Tamil dialects and colloquial forms peculiar to North, Central and Southern Tamilnadu. She also came to Coonoor during the Conference week and spoke to us about the OMF Tamil work in Malaysia. Her last week or two in India were spent at 'Danvi', while I did my best to clarify points of dialect, diction and colloquial usage that had arisen in the places she visited. These were most profitable months for us both.

We had been without a car for a number of years, but then a Mission vehicle became available for our use, a provision that Marty and I much appreciated. Both of us were nearing seventy years of age and were located some distance from Kotagiri town. Moreover the car enabled us to commence literature distribution in villages and Tea or Coffee Estates over a wide area.

A problem of a new kind now faced us. We had acquired a vehicle but had no garage. Friends made various suggestions as to where we should construct a room suitable for this purpose and we finally decided that the best site would be on the western side and attached to the house. The garage was built there and has proved invaluable not only for housing the car but also for keeping tools and numerous other pieces of essential gear.

Paradoxically David's retirement in 1968 led to a wider ministry and influence. He went to Nepal in response to an invitation from friends working there with the United Mission. He preached 'the word of the King' a number of times. Later in 1970 he visited Malaya to help Christian workers among the Tamil speakers. David also met Christian friends who had emigrated there from India, notably Dr G D James who had studied at the Namakkal Mission Boarding School. The two had 'a long chat about the things of God.' There were signs of encouragement through the Tamil radio programmes.

David's energy and devotion to the work were undiminished. "Evangelism is our watchword . . . educational, medical, industrial and other activities can neither be called evangelism nor evangelising agencies unless those engaged in them actually proclaim Christ to the men, women and children with whom they deal."

What follows provides a glimpse into an unobtrusive ministry that David and Marty carried on for a number of years. Evidence suggests that through them the Lord healed a number of people. But there was nothing showy or stage-managed about this. It was kept in strict subordination to the preaching of the gospel. This is another instance of the Throwers' childlike trust in their Lord.

There is also reference to a case of demon-possession. These are controversial matters, of course, which raise many difficult questions. The accounts of them are left here as David Thrower recorded them, without further comment.

6.
New opportunities

The last three months of 1968 were fully occupied for us by a visit that Marty and I paid to the Peninsula Malaysia to help the missionaries of the OMF working among Tamils in that country. The Directors in Singapore had invited us to go over and render some assistance to these workers in their language study and acquaintance with Tamil culture.

Leaving Madras early in October we had a six-day voyage across the Bay of Bengal to Penang Island. We first hugged the Indian coast to Nagapattinam where the vessel stood off-shore for twelve hours while forty-thousand bags of onions were loaded. Apparently each vessel on this run takes a load of onions as Malaysia does not produce that commodity. We were met at Penang, which almost joins the mainland, by a small group of well-wishers including Norma Stewart. The remainder of the year was a full but interesting and satisfying period for us both.

An important item in our programme was a ten day Tamil workshop at the OMF Field Headquarters in Kualal Lumpur. During those days Marty and I gave a total of ten one hour lectures to the Tamil Team of workers on the Tamil language, the Religion of the Tamils, the Tamil Church, how to reach Tamils with the Gospel and Tamil Women – their place in Society and how to present the Gospel to them. Time for discussion was allowed after each lecture and the material was recorded to make it available to a member of the Team who was on Furlough and any future workers among Tamils. On the Sunday of the workshop I preached in one of City's Tamil churches in the morning and in the home of a Tamil Christian family a few miles from Kuala Lumpur later in the day.

Before and after the workshop we visited the members of the team in their stations and gave them as much help, encouragement and advice as possible. Most Sundays I was asked to speak at one or two Tamil services, then by the kindness of the Directors of the Fellowship we had two weeks at the OMF holiday home at an altitude of five thousand feet in the beautiful Cameron Highlands.

The concluding weeks of the visit were spent at Taiping in the north of the country where we were unexpectedly called on for a special kind of service on behalf of a missionary of the fellowship. We were staying with her for a few days when she placed her personal need before us. For a period of four months she had suffered from ulceration of her legs and feet, the irritation of which robbed her of much sleep and handicapped her work. Our friend had tried two doctors, one of whom thought the trouble was an allergy while the other treated it as a fungus. There was no improvement in the condition, and one morning she had to hurry to one of her physicians with the rapidly rising temperature of septicaemia. A large dose of penicillin cured the fever but not the skin infection that caused it. Our friend was strongly opposed to prayer for healing, as she was sure the medical realm was a thing apart. However, by the time of our visit she had suffered so much and could get no relief.

So, when we had prayers one evening, I asked whether she had any special subject for prayer and she exclaimed: "Won't you pray about my skin trouble?" Marty took the ulcerated feet in her hands, while I offered a simple prayer commending our sister's need to the Lord. I concluded by thanking Him for the assurance that He would do the very best for His servant, for whatever the outcome of our

petition might be, it would be the right one. The instant I
pronounced the words, "Thank you, Lord" both Marty and
our friend felt the diseased condition pass from the affected
limbs into the former's hands. No conversation followed.
We just said good-night and went to bed. In the morning
our friend's legs were perfectly healthy down to the ankles.
but the feet were the same as they had been for months. We,
therefore, prayed about the feet the second evening and
thanked God for the blessing He would surely grant His
servant in her need. The next morning both feet were
completely healed except the toes, which showed no sign of
improvement. We repeated the medication the third night
with the result that, when we met our friend in the morning,
she was skipping about and exclaiming: "Come! look at my
feet."

About five years prior to the above incident the Lord
began to lead Marty and me into a quiet, undemonstrative
healing ministry by prayer with laying on of hands. We
worked together in this as a team, usually by request and
almost always after those needing help had done their best
to obtain healing through the medical profession. God's
gracious acts of healing body and mind we regarded as the
gift of implicit faith in His perfect wisdom, love and power,
not as some kind of special endowment of power. Sometimes
months passed without our receiving any requests for this
type of help. At others several persons came to us within a
few days. We always co-operated with the doctors, but at
the same time, advised sufferers to turn to God who made
the human body, first rather than last. We told them to ask
Him whether a doctor should be consulted or an operation
performed.

Our main task was to follow the example of the people
we read about in Mark 2:3 who had faith in Jesus as they
carried a poor paralytic and laid him down in the presence
of Jesus. We do not read that they said anything to the

Lord, yet He did something wonderful for the sufferer. Moreover, He performed the miracle of healing not in response to any faith the man could have exercised in his condition, but He acted on "seeing their faith", the faith of his four bearers. Similarly, He hears and responds to the prayer of faith even today, and two of our Mission colleagues are among those helped by Him through these unworthy and impotent instruments. Both are members of the medical profession, and other doctors and nurses have come to us for the same kind of service from time to time. To Him alone should be rendered praise, for He is the only true Healer. When God graciously designs to use His servants in this way in such a land as Tamilnadu, the results provide powerful demonstrations of what the True God can do.

Apart from assistance rendered to the local Tamil workers in regard to the language I had many opportunities to minister the Word in Taiping, three other meeting places and two rubber estates. Finally, three days after our good friend was relieved of her skin infection we took the train to Kuala Lumpur and thence to Singapore. At the capital of the Island State it was a thrill to step out of the train and be greeted by the name of the station in Tamil as well as English. In Tamil it was the equivalent of Singapuri, the Lion City.

That year appears to have been a exceptionally full one for me, with preaching engagements at Tamil churches around the Nilgiris. There were also many calls for advice or help from individuals needing spiritual, mental or physical ills healed or broken relationships restored. Both of us spent much time visiting homes and we sometimes felt that this service may have been as important and fruitful as our public ministry. Of course we had this kind of involvement in common with most other Christian workers throughout our careers.

On a few occasions we were faced with collapsed marriages. This was a very difficult assignment but, by God's help, we were able to take more than one runaway wife from her parents' home back to her husband. Sometimes we received appeals from persons experiencing well-nigh unbearable conditions of life or work. They needed advice and encouragement. Should they just "Get out of it" or, by the Lord's help, determine to "see it through" till His time of relief or deliverance? It was our joy to see never-to-be-forgotten examples of how God enables His Tamil children to "live down" the most distressing trials. A pastor working with an American Society came to me more than once almost in tears. His situation seemed quite intolerable and he sought my advice. I said to him: "Brother, you know that God has placed you in your sphere of service and you must not run away from it. If you stick it out by His grace, He will vindicate you in due time". That Tamil brother did continue to endure the unendurable, and that for another year or two. He was determined to humble himself under the mighty hand of God, and as a result later come to know the experience of being lifted up, out of despair by God. He came to understand what it meant to cast his anxiety upon the Lord, because He truly cared for him.

The last week of 1969 was full in interest for Marty and me, for it marked our only visit to the southernmost district of Tamilnadu and to Cape Comorin after which the district is named. A Tamil Christian friend of ours who was Principal of a Government-run Secondary School in Kotagiri invited us to his home in Nagercoil, the largest town in that southern area, to attend the wedding of his eldest son. He also invited a Norwegian missionary couple working in Kotagiri. They had one small child. We motored down to Nagercoil and had a very good time with our friends there for four or five days, the only difficulty we experienced being the matter of accommodation. It was the week following Christmas and hotels were full. All the accommodation our host had been able to secure for us was one large room, in the best hotel in the town – for our party of five! However, such problems were not entirely new to us, so we coped alright. We were also shown over India's Space programme a few miles from the city and saw a small piece of rock brought from the moon by American astronauts a few years earlier. On the last Sunday of the year it was my privilege to preach the Word in a thousand seater Tamil church in a town not far from where we were staying. The very large congregation was, no doubt, partly due to that Sunday falling during the Christmas New Year period, a very important festive time for Indian Christians. Arriving home in Kotagiri on 1 January 1970, we had precisely one week of ministry, desk work and packing our bags and then left for furlough in the UK. We had experienced a colourful five years of many differing ministries among Tamils in South India, Malaysia and Singapore. Then we spent about a month touring North India and Nepal, neither of which we had previously visited, and finally embarked at Bombay for the voyage to Britain.

A unique feature of this particular furlough was the holiday that we were able to enjoy for a number of weeks in Scandinavia visiting Norway, Sweden and Denmark. During our years of work in India, we had come to know a wide variety of different people; different nationalities, different languages, different backgrounds, different personalities, but with love for the Lord Jesus Christ, and his work, in common. We were able to renew our fellowship with some of our Scandinavian friends on this holiday, followed by similar occasions in the North of England and in Scotland.

After a heart-warming farewell at our own church in Clapham we left Heathrow for Singapore in mid-November

and began a tour of the Tamil areas of the fellowship in the
Malayan peninsula. It was suggested that we spend our
second week-end in the peninsula with the Tamil group at
Gemas in the south of the country and then work our way
north along the great North-south highway and conclude
the tour in the Taiping area. The Tamil workers had
increased from five to eight since our earlier visit and six of
them were stationed on the Highway, with the remaining
two at Klang only twenty miles from Kuala Lumpur. As we
motored eastward from the west coast we passed through
many miles of rubber plantations at one of which we made a
break to visit a family connected with one of our Tamil
Baptist Churches in Tirunelveli District. We were very
happy to have this unexpected opportunity of calling on
them and they appeared pleased that we had made the
contact with them.

At Gemas Marty and I took part in a variety of
gatherings, but the highlight of the week-end was a service
on Sunday afternoon in the home of Saraswathi's family.
We had contacted this family briefly on our earlier visit to
the country. It consisted of several children and their
widowed mother living in a squalid one-room hovel,
Saraswathi being the oldest of the children and the most
intelligent and mature believer. But on this occasion we
were surprised to find this desperately poor family residing
in an airy, spacious house containing a room big enough to
serve as a meeting place for the local group of Tamil
Christians. What could be the explanation of this dramatic
change?

Well, one day someone noticed a house at the other end
of the town that was empty and going for a remarkably low
rent because the place was haunted and couldn't be let.
Here was a real test of the Christian faith of these folk, for
the terrible power of evil spirits is well-known in Eastern
lands. But Saraswathi and one of her brothers who also was

a staunch believer in the Lord Jesus Christ rose to the challenge thus presented, with the result that the family moved into the haunted house and told all who feared for their safety that the one true God would take care of them, so that they were not afraid of anything in the house. The large room suitable for Sunday services and Gospel outreach was apparently the chief thing about the house that appealed to our friends and it was there I preached the Word that Sunday afternoon. Good publicity was given to the gathering among Tamils in the town and we had a very encouraging attendance. There was no question of the house being haunted then, for the atmosphere brought by its new tenants was such as none of Satan's agents would find to its liking!

It was several hours drive back to Kuala Lumpur with rubber trees, rivers and tin mines filling the area. It was good to renew acquaintance with Tamil friends once more, and particularly one of the workers among them, a Miss Ruth Beckett. The most memorable experience of our few days in Kuala Lumpur was the great joy of meeting Pastor Jacob Paul and his flock, for Jacob Paul was a trophy of saving grace from a village in the Kotagiri section of the Nilgiri's. When he was converted by attending an evangelistic campaign, his life was in danger, his relatives being fiercely anti-Christian Hindus. But some Kotagiri believers protected him until he could escape from the hills. He took theological training, went to Malaysia and became pastor of a Tamil church there. From the Kuala Lumpur centre we moved north to Taiping in the Perak State. There we stayed several weeks ministering and were taken care of by two lady Tamil workers who live in a Malay tin-mining village a couple of miles outside the town. This arrangement provided ideal conditions for us to assist these sisters with their Tamil problems. In addition, I was also to give the message at a Tamil service on Sundays in the town church on several occasions. Marty and I also visited a number of Tamil homes.

The Overseas Missionary Fellowship Directors generously gave us a fortnight's holiday at their bungalow in the cool of the Cameron Highlands as they did during our earlier visit. While we were at the Bungalow we received an unexpected request to speak at a Gospel meeting for the Tamils of a village a short distance away. A Western couple who knew little or no Tamil were burdened for these people and, learning of our visit to the hills, arranged the meeting, although they were somewhat doubtful regarding my Tamil being intelligible to those folk. In the event we had about a score of Tamil shop-keepers, their families and others along. After the programme concluded I asked one of the women: "Did you understand what I said?" She gave this reply: "I understood your language alright, but how could I understand your message? I never heard anything like that before!"

When we arrived back in Tamilnadu in February 1971 we had travelled at least the equivalent of a round-the-world tour since we left Madras for Calcutta thirteen months earlier.

When we finally ended our wanderings by driving home to 'Danvi', we enjoyed the fruits of the fine job that one of our colleagues had done for us during our absence. He had given our vintage 'Standard Ten' vehicle to the 'Ooty' agents for a thorough overhaul and we much appreciated his help in this way. Marty and I shared the driving for the eighteen miles of very tortuous mountain roads so that both of us could sample and test our 'new' car.

One of the first things we had to inspect was the permanent building constructed for the Kotagiri Christian Book Centre during our absence. Our friend Signe Anderson had supervised the work of the bookshop throughout that year and we were happy and thankful to find that she was willing and able to continue to carry this responsibility on a permanent basis. For obvious reasons Marty and I could not continue the work much longer, the building was only a few yards from Signe's house and she had just had a year's experience. We for our part continued to distribute Christian literature in the villages and tea or coffee estates of the rural area around us, and to a much wider field in response to orders received through the post.

March 1971 saw us in Madras again; this time we went just for a day or two to see our heavy luggage from Britain, which was coming by sea, through Customs. Whilst waiting for the ship's arrival, I had invitations to preach at Vepery and Mannur on the Sundays. But we had also heard that Pastor M Daniel, of the Tamil Baptist church in Tiruverkadu and a friend of nearly fifty years standing, was not well. So we went to see him and found him greatly in need of encouragement. He was sitting in a chair and explained that he could not walk or even stand without assistance. Our brother must have been in a weak state for some time, for a report was in circulation that his days of active service were ended. Marty and I were deeply touched by his pathetic condition and tenderly commended our friend and colleague to the Lord in prayer. Then Marty helped Daniel to his feet and took him for a short walk in the forecourt of the adjoining chapel. She also said to him: "We have asked the Lord to give you the strength you need, so you must use all that He gives you." As she sat him in his chair again, she added: "As you look to the Lord for His strengthening touch take a stroll like this every day. You have shown us that you can do it, and remember to add a pace or two each time."

A few weeks later we had a letter from Pastor Daniel saying that he was somewhat stronger and had conducted a communion service for his church. After another month or two he wrote again, this time telling us that he was leading the services in his chapel and also visiting nearby villages for Gospel work, and he continued to serve the church for a further decade.

Demon possession is lamentably common in this country and is easily distinguished from mental disorder. In May 1971 Marty and I became involved in the case of a young woman living in a village three miles from Kotagiri. She had been possessed by a demon called Palaniswamy for nine months and her guardian wished her delivered.

First he went to a priest of his own religion, but the Hindu priest failed to exorcise the evil spirit. Then the man remembered the missionary whom he knew and sought his help, for he was sure the Christian's God would be able to deliver his niece. The missionary contacted a Tamil pastor with experience of this type of case and arranged for him to go to the Mission bungalow and perform the exorcism the following Sunday afternoon. He then came to us and requested us to go to his place that Sunday and give this woman, her uncle and other members of her family some teaching regarding what the pastor was going to do for them. He came to Marty and me because he did not speak Tamil. We, therefore, went and spoke to this family about the implications of their seeking the help and blessing of the true and living God in this time of their need. I also read to them the New Testament record of two cases of demon possession that the Lord Jesus dealt with during His earthly ministry, which bore a remarkable resemblance to this case, in several ways.

Then we were ready for the good offices of the Tamil pastor who had promised to take over the proceedings. but he hadn't arrived! We waited a few minutes and then as he was still delayed, we had perforce to carry on the task in hand without him. I knew I was in for the fiercest spiritual conflict of my life and one for which I was totally unprepared. Fear gripped me, not that the Lord Jesus would fail, but that I would fail Him. But I took up the awe-inspiring challenge and, in a loud voice, I commanded Palaniswamy in the name of the Lord Jesus Christ the Son of the Living God to leave the woman and never enter her again. The girl became very uncomfortable and began to weep. Marty tried to comfort her. Then the uncle announced that the demon was still there. The four or five of us who were in on this were greatly distressed and fell on our knees crying to the Lord to honour His holy name. We pleaded with Him to show His divine power and not permit the Enemy to make capital out of the incident.

After we had prayed a few minutes the young woman's uncle sent to her and asked her name. The demon then gave its name, "Palaniswamy." A Tamil conversation between the two ensued more or less as follows: "Why are you refusing to leave, although you have been ordered to do so in the name of Jesus Christ?" "You troubled me like this a week ago, telling me to leave this woman. I told you that I would go after two weeks. You have only given me one week up to to-day. I will quit after eight more days" (the Tamil way of referring to a week.) Those last words were my signal for further action, so I sprang to my feet and went and stood by the woman. I then repeated the order to Palaniswamy in these words: "We are not giving you eight days, not eight hours or even eight minutes. In the name of Jesus Christ the Son of the Living God I command you to leave this woman NOW". As I pronounced that final word with great sternness and determination, the afflicted girl opened her eyes, instantly delivered and perfectly normal, and whenever we meet this young woman or any of her family we are assured that she is well and worships no deity but Jesus.

We spent Christmas 1971 at home in Kotagiri with Miss Rosamund Oxlade of the South Africa General Mision, whom we met at Durban on our way to Britain early the previous year. Rosamund had a great desire to assist in promoting Gospel outreach to the Tamil community of South Africa and, with this in view, was paying a visit to Tamilnadu to see something of the Tamils in their own land. Two days later Rosamund accompanied us as we left the hills and went to Madras by car for a couple of weeks holiday.

At that period much of my time was occupied with the preparation of a more or less verse-by-verse Tamil commentary on the Minor Prophets. This work was eventually published in two small volumes containing, in addition to the commentary, an introduction to each book, chronological table, maps and copious indexes of subjects and scripture references. The commentary was the culmination of a quarter of a century of work on this portion of the Bible. First there were eighteen pamphlets of study notes for use in Bible classes, which later were twice issued in book form. Later still, in response to a request from the Evangelical Fellowship of India, I wrote a commentary on the Minor Prophets in English, which was to be translated into eight of India's chief languages for use by book clubs in these languages. Finally, I put all the material into Tamil and had it printed. Shortly after the second volume was issued I received great encouragement in the shape of an order for one hundred copies of each book from my colleagues in Madras who often contact theological students in the City.

Whilst in India, and especially during the later years, we were able to enjoy a number of visits by folk from Britain, in connection with mission. Imagine how pleased we were when at the close of 1972, a partial family reunion occurred, when Vivian and his son, Paul were able to visit us. We enjoyed something of a mini tour around some of the interesting parts of South India, our old and battered

'Standard Ten' managing to cover the thousand miles or so of the round trip, very well. The Wild Life Sanctuary was of special interest to our visitors, for it contains large numbers of wild elephants, two or three varieties of deer, many herds of gaur (wild oxen commonly called bison), wild pig, an occasional tiger, monkeys, peacocks. The early morning tour of the jungle on a tame elephant was not new to Marty and me but it was a great treat for our visitors who saw some of these animals in their natural habitat.

After our visitors had gone the Mission Book Depot of Dindigul was closed and it was decided to dispose of as much of our stock of literature as possible to other similar distributing agencies and transfer the remainder to a one-room cottage in the Danvi compound. Consequently, book cases, steel shelving and stocks of books were received here during the month of April. As few of our publications have been reissued since that time, while distribution has continued, the stock held here at 'Danvi' has steadily decreased year by year. Our present residual stock requires no more than two bookcases.

Around the turn of the year Marty and I were back in the capital of the Tamil country, waiting for a visitor to arrive, whose precise date of travel was not known. We visited a number of the Tamil Baptist churches and I gave messages in some of them. I also had the rare experience of preaching in Tamil at a Telugu church in the City. One third of the population of Madras are Telegus but most of them know enough Tamil to understand what is said in that language. So I was asked to use Tamil and thus avoid the necessity for interpretation which is usually an unsatisfactory, make-shift affair.

On our return we enjoyed a perfect run and I said a silent word of praise to God as I switched off the engine in our garage. I must add that I personally had only driven from Kotagiri town where we dropped our driver, who we had greatly needed, at his home! Sunday 2nd March that year was an important date in our calendar, for that was the day I would be travelling to Coimbatore in the late evening to meet Irwin, who was expected to arrive in the early hours. He had by this time made a vast improvement in his health and was coming to serve God in the land of his birth.

I started soon after nightfall, picked up my driver Isaac in Kotagiri and handed over to him for the rest of the journey. We reached the bottom of the ghat road and entered the plains about 8.30 pm. A few hundred yards further on we approached a group of three galloping animals like outsized cows hurtling ahead of us on the left side of the road, obviously scared of our headlights. Isaac called out "Yanai!" (Elephants!) I at once told him to stop the car, turn off the lights and remain silent. He responded promptly but not soon enough to avoid landing ourselves in grievous peril.

As our eyes became accustomed to the darkness we caught sight of the male elephant standing near the car. How enormous he looked compared with our small vehicle! Where would we be if he decided to use that great trunk or those fearsome tusks on us! We had stopped not a second too soon, as we were now between the male and the rest of the herd.

The fugitives up the road were apparently his mate and her two almost full grown calves. The great beast beside us was scarcely visible in the darkness. This was evidently 'it' for us, for the infuriated animal would almost certainly crush the little tin box and its occupants with one foot, as easily as we would break a match-box. It was only by the mercy of God in controlling this powerful animal that the elephant remained quiet and unperturbed, slowly walking past the car, crossing the road in front of us and joining the rest of the herd.

In 1975 Tamilnadu and southern Andhra just to the
north of Tamilnadu, suffered one of the most disastrous
droughts in living memory. Rain eluded the whole of the
Tamil country, and the Nilgiri District appears to have
been one of the most severely affected areas. These
conditions had persisted for two years and the great
reservoir that supplies Madras city completely dried up and
the water works only succeeded in supplying a little water to
the people every other day by hurriedly sinking a large
number of borer wells. Here at 'Danvi' even our well failed
for a time because it was not deep enough to tap any of the
three springs traced by the dowsers to that spot but at a
great depth. We, therefore, deepened the well and struck
water six feet deeper, but we still have a well that is less
than half the depth of any other on this the Golden Hill, all
of which were dry at that time. What a gracious provision
the Lord has made for His unworthy servant here!

My annual engagement to speak at the Harvest
Thanksgiving services at Ootacamund Baptist church came
round as usual the second Saturday in October. That year
we arrived late as our accelerator wire snapped seven miles
short of 'Ooty'. For a few moments my driver and I
wondered what we could do regarding the problem thus
created. Then I suggested prayer for guidance and we spent
a few moments asking God to help us, for we were on His
business. Then I started the engine, put it in first gear and
found that the vehicle would run, albeit very slowly up the
steep road and we reached the church just before it was my
turn to give the address. A new accelerator cable was fitted
at an Ooty garage before the meeting was over.

Practically the whole of December we took as a real
holiday in Madras. The 22nd of the month was the fiftieth
Anniversary of that day when David Thrower wedded
Martena Watts in Sendamangalam. We had a very quiet
celebration in our room at the Guest House with Irwin and

two Indian friends. After a special tea with "wedding cake" and a few other such items we had a time of thanksgiving to Him who had granted us half a century of united life and service for Him in Tamilnadu, with 'mercies countless as the sands', day by day all the way along.

Later we received a telegram telling us that our colleague Pastor Samuel Devanesam of Kilpauk, Madras had died while visiting one of his sons in North India. This was a sad blow to us, for our brother was a long-standing personal friend of ours and also one of the most valuable workers in Tamilnadu. Thus this servant of God was buried many miles from home with none of his family present apart from the son he was visiting. A day or two after the telegram, I received a letter from the Kilpauk church secretary, pleading with me to go to the city and preside at a Memorial service the next Sunday afternoon in spite of the great heat of Madras at that time of year. It was not an easy decision to reach but I decided that I should respond to this appeal providing I could secure transport by plane from Coimbatore. Although there was no travel agent in Kotagiri I was able to make suitable bookings of flights by Indian Airlines for that week-end. In the event all went well and, apart from an hour of discomfort around noon on the Sunday, I did not suffer unduly from the heat. An estimated five hundred persons were present at the service but they were easily accommodated in the Kilpauk chapel which had been enlarged a few months earlier. A particularly pleasing item in the programme was a special hymn sung by our departed brother's eight children. The service was a great comfort to the members of the church and many others who esteemed him highly and valued his ministry. I personally was deeply grateful that I was invited and enabled to take part in this service.

David is now 76 and Marty 78, and Marty's health begins to cause concern. David nursed her in increasingly trying circumstances until her death in November 1980 at 'Danvi', the bungalow that David had been delighted to be able to buy for his retirement.

Yet even these years of 'quiet retirement' were not without turmoil. The Throwers were burgled, and beaten-up in the process. By God's goodness they were able to pray for their enemies and to rejoice together in God's deliverance of them. 'Always giving thanks to God the Father for everything' was a strong theme of David's in these later years. Like the Apostle Paul, David and Marty knew what it is to be in need and what it is to have plenty. During what was to be his last visit to England in 1982 David was able to view his own advanced age calmly and without bitterness.

David Thrower was one of the last of a line of devoted missionaries to India. During the last thirty years of his long life the responsibility for the oversight of the churches passed increasingly and eventually completely into Indian hands while the work of the Mission there became increasigly concentrated on radio and literature evangelism. These changes David Thrower – with his enterprising spirit, his concern for literature, and above all his jelousy for the work of the gospel in India – heartily endorsed.

7.
Always giving thanks

After what was quite literally a 'flying visit' to Madras in June, life and work went on fairly normally here at 'Danvi', although I became increasingly concerned regarding Marty's health. She had several black-outs and falls about that time and needed help more frequently than before. Also in that year, Marty began to experience increasing difficulty with her speech and I remember one occasion when she tried to say something to me that I could not understand. This trial, which eventually led to her complete loss of this means of communication, was probably the greatest limitation she suffered during her last two years. Moreover, those of us who tried to help her, shared her suffering in this matter, for we were completely frustrated by our inability to discover what she needed or how she felt.

Then the most outstanding date for us in that year's calendar dawned – Tuesday 17 August 1976. We had prayed long and earnestly for help in the home. Marty could not continue catering and caring for the home much longer. We tried to find someone suitable and a woman came for a time, but we had to dispense with her services. Then we realised afresh that the needs of God's servants are best supplied by Him. Thus the Lord prepared us for what He had ready that Tuesday in the middle of August.

That day our mail brought a letter from Ruth Beckett of the Overseas Missionary Fellowship team of workers among Tamils in Malaysia. We had not heard from her for a considerable time, so we were eager to get news of the Lord's work the other side of the bay of Bengal. Oh yes, she had news for us and what amazing news it was! She informed us that the Lord had definitely told her to come and care for her 'Mum and Dad' Thrower in their old age. Here was God's gracious answer to our cries for help. Ruth was a trained and experienced nurse who knew us and our situation, having visited us here. But what about her work for the OMF? The Malaysian Government disposed of that by terminating her visit pass as from the end of the year, on completely spurious grounds.

6 January 1977 was the day we met Ruth at Kotagiri Post Office as she lighted from the mail bus that had brought her up from Mettupalayam, after her journey from Kuala Lumpur. She quickly settled into the routine of the house and relieved Marty of all household duties. We could not express in words our profound thankfulness and gratitude to the Lord for sending her and to Ruth for her willingness to be sent to our aid at that difficult time in our career.

A friendship soon developed between Ruth and Irwin, culminating in their marriage in June of that year. Everyone was happy that Marty was able to attend the service, although she did not feel well enough to join us at the reception afterwards. This was indeed to be the last occasion that she was able to attend any place of worship.

For some time, the Lord had been teaching us the significance of Ephesians 5:20, which reads "Always giving thanks to God the Father for everything in the name of our Lord Jesus Christ", together with a little of the blessedness of doing what it says. How often it is that our joy in the Lord and our thanksgiving to Him are adversely affected by changing circumstances and unhappy events! Our joy, however, should be grounded in the character of God and the truth we read about Him, and He never changes! Our thanksgiving should be found in the mercy and goodness that God shows to us His children and in the absolute control he has over the circumstances surrounding our lives – and all things are for our good!

On the morning of Sunday 18 December 1977, I preached at the Kotagiri Baptist church and the day appears to have been quite normal for all of us at 'Danvi'. Marty and I retired around 9 pm., and were soon asleep. The next thing I knew was Irwin standing beside me, and oh, the pain! My head beaten, my hands smashed. Blood everywhere. But what of Marty?

At about 10.30 pm an intruder entered the house, and came into our bedroom looking for money. First he rendered Marty and me unconscious by beating us on the head with a rough piece of wood from one of our trees. Providentially Irwin and Ruth heard our cries and ran to our help. Irwin entered our room just as the assailant was leaving the house by a door.

Mercifully Marty was not so badly injured as I was, but her lacerated head needed eight stitches and she was greatly shaken by the incident. A surgeon living in an adjoining compound was called and rendered first aid, but of that I was completely unaware. Irwin reported the matter to the police and made arrangements for us to be admitted to the local Christian hospital which happens to be the nearest medical institution. I was unconscious during all this but recovered my intelligence shortly before the ambulance arrived. As I opened my eyes I saw Irwin standing beside me and, without waiting a second to collect my wits, I called out: "Irwin! We must thank God for this and pray for the culprit". Those words must have been from above, for it is not in the heart of man to say "Thank you, Father" at such a time as that. Marty and I were hospitalised for eighteen days, receiving skilled and loving treatment from every member of the staff that handled our case, many of whom were already long-standing friends of ours. Thanking God for the beating-up no doubt helped both of us to keep cheerful throughout those trying days. One day the Superintendent of the hospital expressed his surprise that I was so 'humorous', to which I quickly explained: "Oh, Doctor, I've got two of them, one in each arm".

After we returned home during the first week of January, it soon became clear that I would have to devolve some of my commitments without delay, including the Field Treasurership of the Mission.

From the beginning of 1978 Marty had to spend more and more time in bed and also progressively lost the ability to walk without assistance. I had some time previously been given a wheel-chair to keep 'until someone needs it'. This became extremely useful, enabling Marty to have some time in the garden whenever weather permitted. In fact I wheeled her in the garden for an hour the last afternoon she remained with us. But her strength gradually declined until, for the last eighteen months, she was unable to do anything for herself. While she could still speak she often asked me to sing to her and I sometimes sang as many as seven of our favourite hymns. I usually sang to her on Sundays in any case, and had a brief time of devotions with her. One day early that year I read Psalm 23 to her and she repeated the verses after me. We did this on several occasions and one day, when I reached words, "He restoreth my soul", Marty repeated the line and added: "He has done that for me".

For a time she had been distressed because she felt she could not pray. So that day we praised the Lord together for restoring and strengthening her spirit. It was gracious of Him to do this just when she was finding it difficult to submit patiently to the many limitations that were her lot. Another day she remarked to me that she had cried to the Lord and He had strengthened her. At that time I noted that she really appeared to be stronger. If I have given the impression that Marty, and more particularly I, generally maintained a positive and thankful reaction to the varied experiences that came our way I must correct that. A few weeks after our beating up both of us passed through a time of deep depression, pulling each other down instead of up! But I am thankful to say that the Lord helped us so that it was not very long before we both escaped from the 'Slough of Despond'. Throughout our married life, Marty was more steady and philosophical in facing difficult situations than I.

Not all was heavy going at this time, however, for one evening late in July a strange apparition appeared at the front door of our house. It was a noisy one too! I ran out to see what it was and found an auto-rickshaw with a trailer containing a large packing-case. Whatever could it mean? These vehicles, with their tiny engines, are normally found in large towns and used as taxis, but never for transport to the hills. No wonder the driver complained that he arrived later than he had hoped, because his machine had difficulty in climbing that mountain road! A man accompanying the driver explained that he had come from Salem and had brought a refrigerator that the Field Treasurer of the Mission had purchased and instructed him to deliver to me here. He unloaded the case, unpacked the machine and put this magnificent gift to work in our kitchen, where it has since given trouble-free service.

We later received word from our Secretary in Britain to the effect that the gift of this regrigerator was made on the suggestion of members of Council as a token of their appreciation of our long fellowship in the Lord's service in Tamilnadu and particularly in recognition of my quarter of a century as Field Treasurer. This was a heart-touching gesture, deeply appreciated by us both and received at a time when much encouragement was needed. It has also given us a daily reminder of the remarkable industrial progress India has made during the past few decades.

Moreover, the gift could not have taken a more useful form, for which we have constant cause to be grateful.

A matter of a very different kind which, instead of requiring a few hours to complete, became a more or less continual preoccupation of many months during 1978 was the aftermath of the 'Danvi' break-in. First there were the police enquiries, statements and fingerprints. Then in April the intruder was caught breaking into another house. Finally, in the late summer, the superintendent of the hospital, Irwin and I had to go to 'Ooty' twice to give evidence at the hearing of the case in the Sessions Court. The accused, a young man of twenty-two, was found guilty of house-breaking and theft with assault and given two years of probation as his sentence. We wished him no ill; only blessing from Him whose servants he had attacked.

One day in October Marty was sitting on the front verandah and noticed the car, which was standing in the forecourt. She, to our surprise, indicated that she would like to go out in it. So we took her to a small but beautiful park a couple of miles from here and were pleased to find that she was able to sit up in the car and enjoy the drive and the flowers, which can be seen from the road. We therefore repeated such short outings a few times at intervals, a practise which became seriously hindered, for in that particular year we had a bumper monsoon during which the 'Danvi' rain guage recorded fifteen inches of rain within a period of twenty-four hours. That November a cyclone caused a landslide that washed away part of a Badega village, four miles from Kotagiri, resulting in the loss of several lives. The wind uprooted or broke many trees in our compound.

On the evening of our wedding anniversary just before Christmas Marty gave me a thrill. When I said "good-night" to her she managed to say "Thank-you". Despite Marty's gradual decline, I was enabled to continue some work at this time and during March and April 1979 yet another new experience came my way. I had been given a General Power of Attorney in 1942 but it had never fallen to my lot to represent the Mission in a court of law. As more than a decade had elapsed since all properties in India had been legally transferred to indigenous Tamil Baptist Church Trusts it appeared that I would escape that experience altogether. However, early in 1979 the Madras Trust members requested me to help them in connection with a court case brought by a person who claimed ownership of the Church and school property of the Trust in one of the Madras villages. Our colleagues serving on the Trust pointed out that I was the only person with sufficient personal knowledge of the Mission's ownership and use of property in question. I, therefore, acceded to the request and flew to Madras that March to testify at the hearing of the case in the court in Poonamallee. But on arrival in the city I learned that the lawyer for the plaintiff had been granted an extension of time to prepare his case. I flew back and awaited a second call. The following month I was again in court, only to be informed that this witness would not be called till three days later. On our second visit to the court we again waited a few hours before I was sent for and led to the witness box, where I spent the next hour and more, where I was requested to give my evidence in Tamil instead of English as is usual in the case of foreigners. The judge demurred when he heard this proposal but finally agreed after the lawyer had assured him that I could cope with Tamil alright. The case was at last won by the Trust and the property retained for the use of the Tamil Baptist church in the village.

In total contrast to this, I also undertook the supervision of some building work during the course of the year. Living accommodation is extremely difficult to secure in Kotagiri, particularly by the poorer section of the population. This problem is a chronic and recurring one, as we ourselves experienced at 'Mistley' bungalow many years before. At this later period it was the families of our two house helps who were affected and we decided to erect two small houses for their occupation, if we could find suitable plots of ground available at a reasonable price. Much prayer was made regarding this need and its financial implications. In October 1979, having secured the land at a remarkably reasonable price, we laid foundations for the house in square granite blocks – there is an abundance of granite in Kotagiri. This work was done shortly before the North East Monsoon and the foundations were then left to become consolidated by the heavy rains. The rooms were constructed during the dry months of early 1980.

For a period of twelve months from March 1980 I had the services of a real secretary for the first time in my life. His assistance was invaluable, particularly as he had a Theology degree and therefore was at home in the Greek New Testament and Septuagint. As soon as he joined me here I began dictating the early chapters of this story to him for typing. I also dictated articles for Tamil and English magazines which Daniel then finalised for me. We also engaged in a certain amount of biblical research together, and undertood small Tamil and English printing tasks. So it was that I continued to be very busy during Marty's last months. Not only did I spend many hours nursing and caring for her, but I was involved at various times in such activities as teaching and preaching, writing and printing, accountancy and legal work, theology and building work. Such has been the many sided nature of my life and work.

In October Marty developed congestion of the lungs for which she was treated and to a certain extent responded to the medication. However, early in November the congestion became worse, but when the doctor strolled up to 'Danvi' just to see how we were getting on, he thought Marty was a

little better than when he saw her a few days earlier. My
helpers and I saw little change in her condition at that time.
So I gave her the usual hour in the garden on Friday
afternoon. But we did observe that her face had shed signs
of strain or discomfort and appeared to be more bright than
we had ever seen it. Then a simple yet remarkable change
occurred in our household routine. Once a week, on Fridays
it was our custom to hold our daily household prayers in the
bedroom around Marty's bed. That week, however, it was
not possible for me to be present on Friday and we decided
to postpone the bedroom session till Saturday morning.
Thus, about 10 am on Saturday 8 November our helpers
and I gathered for a brief time of devotions in the bedroom
and,although it was not my turn to lead the prayer, I was
requested to do so.

Almost immediately afterwards Marty was taken to the
front verandah and given her mid-morning cup of coffee.
She was sitting in the bright sunshine and, shortly after
drinking the coffee, lifted her head, opened her eyes and
looked up towards heaven. Then she gave a shout and was
with her Lord into whose hands we had commended her
half an hour before. It is my unshakable conviction that this
was a glorious end to a life that had the will of our heavenly
Father as its paramount concern at all times. I think each
member of the household was deeply impressed and greatly
comforted by the way we had been led that morning.

Immediately after Marty's sudden translation I called
the doctor who was disappointed that he was too late (as he
put it) to help Marty, but he graciously went in person and
informed our chief Kotagiri friends. That Sunday morning,
Pastor Victor Benjamin, came over from 'Ooty' and
conducted a heart-warming service at 'Danvi' in Tamil
about noon that day. In the afternoon Kotagiri Union Hall
had a congregation of about one hundred and twenty for the
thanksgiving and funeral service, during which three of

Marty's favourite hymns were sung. Then about seventy folk joined us at the briefer committal service at the cemetery. Many folk travelled a long way and at very short notice to share in my grief at Marty's passing, after nearly fifty-five years of marriage, and to share in thanksgiving to God for a lifetime spent in devotion and love to Jesus Christ.

Three days after the above events I was taken to Madras for a couple of weeks rest. It was great to be able to relax and have a nap whenever I felt like it! Then I returned home to face the many adjustments demanded by my new situation. By God's help most of the problems were satisfactorily solved before Christmas, when my 'normal' vacation was once again enjoyed in the big city that I knew so well, the home and haunts of Marty and me for so many years in the now distant past.

It may seem strange for me to undertake a second trip to Madras less than a month after returning from the previous one, particularly as each such visit involves upwards of seven hundred miles travel. But I had little option as some engagements had been booked months earlier and there were other important and interesting items in store for me that just could not be missed. For on the second Sunday of that month I took part in a special service at Kilpauk for the dedication of Samuel Devanesam junior to the pastoral office.

It was an inspiring occasion, with the chapel packed by a congregation of about five hundred. The programme was a lengthy one that occupied two and a half hours.

On returning to 'Danvi', I began to spend several hours at Queens Hill, a missionary guest home about twenty minutes walk from 'Danvi', every Sunday by going there for lunch, a siesta and tea after attending one of the churches for the morning service. This prevents my becoming a complete hermit up here at 'Danvi' and also provides contact with fellow-guests from all over the sub-continent and beyond. But apart from these interludes, my simple routine rotated uneventfully throughout the year. There were occasional opportunities to preach at the local Tamil Baptist Church and, in October, the standing order to speak at the Ootacamund church Harvest Thanksgiving.

At that time I also received what seemed to me a rather incongruous request. The minister of a Tamil church at a village nearly thirty miles from here, on the Western side of the Nilgiri's came to Kotagiri to ask me to speak at a special service for his young people, at which the youth of the church would take part. When I demurred, asking the pastor why he was calling an octogenarian to speak at a youth service he replied, "Ayya! it's your experience we want our young folk to benefit of". It was a Sunday morning service and I had a very happy time with the young people, giving a simple lesson from the School of Christ.

Over a number of months, I had repeatedly been asked to make a tenth visit to the United Kingdom, and I had vaguely envisaged such an excursion around the end of 1982. Then I learned that Yvonne Conacher, one of my missionary colleagues, would be taking a three-month furlough in Britain that Spring and, while I was not enamoured of the thought of undertaking a semi trans-world tour alone, here was a bandwaggon too good to miss! So we travelled together on an Air India excursion, leaving Madras early in March and returning in the opening days of June. The outward flight was for me a record as we travelled from Madras to London in a little under sixteen hours.

That return to the Old Country was made a decade too late for it to be completely enjoyable to me. Being indulged upon in my eighties, it was unavoidably somewhat like the proverbial curate's egg, good in parts. For example, I found the English climate in March rather grim while, at the same time, the exquisite beauty of the early Spring provided a more than ample compensation. Again, crossing the road without getting knocked down was an art to be relearned. Happily, I enjoyed the full use of 'shank's Mare', and gave it plenty of exercise, particularly on many of the ramblers' walks in Suffolk.

During the time I was in Britain I took in a variety of meetings, an average of once every week, in Surrey, London, Essex and Suffolk. All were times of happy fellowship and sharing of the Word of God, but the most outstanding was the Church Anniversary of the spiritual home where I was baptized in the year 1916 – Courland Grove Baptist Church, Clapham. That delightful reunion took place on Good Friday. The greatest joy of that occasion was the opportunity it provided for me to express in person my gratitude for all the faithful friendship and unwavering suppport received from my church all these sixty six years.

Yvonne and I left London during an English heat wave on 3 June and arrived in Madras during an Indian one, with the temperature just below 108°F. After a weekend in the City I came home and tried to settle into my quite life here at 'Danvi' again. This latter took a while, of course. However, I was soon occupying Tamil pulpits occasionally, writing articles for Tamil magazines, supervising literature distribution and the launching of the 'Danvi' reading courses for children.

As I look back on the six decades I have been in Tamilnadu the experience and activities of those years stir my heart to thank God for them all. Like the prophet Isaiah I have to tell my Master "Lord . . . all that we have accomplished you have done for us".

Among other things, I have tried to learn that all our experiences, including those related to our work and witness, are part of our training for God's service at a later time. I have long felt that Hebrews 12:5-11 teaches one of the most important lessons for believers, for the original

Greek word used so many times in that passage and generally rendered 'chastisement' or 'discipline' in the English versions basically refers to the training of children. Although the original significance of the term was the education and training of the young, unfortunately in the case of God's children this all too often has to take the form of disciplinary action and even chastisement. But, as the last verse of that passage in Hebrews states, great blessing accrues to those who are 'trained' by His loving, disciplining hand. Well disciplined followers are the only mature disciples. Marty and I sometimes found Tamilnadu a rigorous training ground, but neither of us wished to change it for an easier one.

In addition, we have seen that even more important than our service as Christians, are our lives. Our walk is more important than our work, our reaction to what happens to us more potent for good than our service. Ezekiel emphasised this, when he wrote that God had this to say to the people of his day, "The nations will know that I am the Lord . . . when I show myself holy through you before their eyes". That divine statement regarding the outreach of His saving truth to all peoples is as relevant now as it was in the prophet's time. In other words, the most effective factor in all gospel witness is the life of the believer. Although much illiteracy still exists in many lands no normal human being is unable to 'read' the daily life of a Christian.

From Tamilnadu, the land of my calling and adoption, I dedicate my simple testimony. By God's grace and goodness He has immeasurably enriched my life through fellowship with many of my Tamil brothers and sisters. But what of the prospect? That is as gloriously bright as all the "great and precious promises" of God. There must be no looking back. "Brothers! one thing I do: forgetting what is behind and straining towards what is ahead, I press on towards the goal for which God has called me".

Postscript

In February 1985 Peter Day and Chris Richards, President and Secretary of Grace Baptist Mission (formerly Strict Baptist Mission) had the privilege of visiting David Thrower in Kotagiri. They were able to enjoy a precious time of fellowship together, tinged with sadness since all three sensed that as they parted it would be for the last time on this earth. David was still active in the Lord's work at that time, busily preparing Bible Reading notes for the Tamil Baptist magazine; still having occasional opportunities to preach.

He was about to receive treatment locally for a facial scar. In the event the problem proved more complicated than at first appeared and necessitated travelling to Madras for radium treatment. He stayed in the home of his colleagues, Yvonne Conacher and Olive Knight. On Saturday 13 July 1985 they noted that he did not take his usual daily walk. Very early the next morning Yvonne went to rouse David with a refreshing drink. He drank and then passed peacefully into the presence of the Lord whom he had served so diligently for so long. Olive Knight wrote "What a blessed Sunday for him!"

It was sixty three and a half years since David first arrived in India. For him there had been no looking back. Our prayer is that the example of a life thus lived for the Lord may challenge many today to glorify God in a life of missionary service.